Cycling's 50 Craziest Stories

Cycling's 50 Craziest Stories

Les Woodland

Published by McGann Publishing
P.O. Box 576
Cherokee Village, AR 72525
USA
www.mcgannpublishing.com

McGann
Publishing

ISBN 978-0-9843117-1-2
Printed in the United States of America

For Stéphanie, my French wife

Table of Contents

Introduction

Crazy Sport, Crazy Guys

All sports have their funny stories. But some are funnier than others because some sports are inherently crazier. In soccer, for instance, there were goalkeepers who leaned against the posts and smoked a cigarette when the game went down to the other end of the pitch. But soccer's funny stories don't go much further than people shooting for goal and hitting the crowd instead.

There are wonderful characters in boxing, maybe the only sport that comes close to cycling for attracting both poor boys anxious to escape the slums or the backbreaking work of farms or mines and the shady, half-educated men prepared to help them do it for a cut of the rewards. But there aren't actually many funny stories about boxing itself, because boxing is about having the stuffing knocked out of you by someone bigger and stronger and it's hard to get a good laugh out of that.

Cycling, on the other hand, is not only a sport but a journey. Races go from one place to another and by improbable routes. And as anyone knows who has tried to make a complicated and roundabout train journey on a Sunday morning, travel by improbable routes is fraught with problems. Journeys are slower than they're supposed to be, or trains are diverted down backwoods routes to help engineers working on the main line, or they stop without explanation in rural stations that you've never heard of.

See the connection with cycling? For roundabout journeys and improbable breakdowns, think of the mountains. For soul-destroying delays, think of punctures and what the French call *la fringale*, that sudden and death-inducing suffering that comes from riding too far and eating too little. Compared to that, a rattling, stuffy and noisy country train seems distinctly luxurious.

Of course, what makes it all the more fun, is that cycling is *supposed* to be uncomfortable. The more a race has the power to make its riders thoroughly miserable, the greater its allure becomes. Flat races on smooth roads are dismissed as boring. Stick in several hours of Europe's biggest mountains or take the race down the filthiest, man-ruining roads you can find in northern France or Belgium and we get misty-eyed at the romance of it all. Even the riders seem to enjoy it. For every rider like Bernard Hinault who refused to ride races like the Tour of Flanders because they were "a dangerous lottery", there are a hundred who want no more than to put their mud-stiffened and torn-shouldered jersey behind glass and hang it in their homes after winning Paris–Roubaix.

Well, we know the winners of Paris–Roubaix and the other great races. For them, things often went as smoothly as they could, eased along the road by the best domestiques and managers that money could buy. We admire their victories and wish we could be half as good, we who go out on our bikes on Sunday mornings and dream of being gods.

But what of the times when things went wrong, not just for the stars but for those whose only stake in history is the misery or absurdity they briefly went through? What of the sport's craziest moments, the riders who tried to win a classic by coming through the wrong door, the man who defied nature and bladder with a length of rubber, the humble team rider who was pushed to his yellow jersey like a man to the guillotine?

Let us celebrate them. Let us revel in the absurdity of a sport we consider the best in the world. And let us feel happy that whatever else happens, there will always be something equally improbable just around the corner…

Happy … and problem-free … cycling!

St-Maurin, France

Les Woodland

1

HOW TO WIN A RACE ... BY LESS THAN A TIRE

When Henri Desgrange wrote a book about tactics, he called it *Heads and Legs*. He knew what he was talking about. You need more than just big thighs to win a bike race.

Take Charles Terront, for instance. You don't get craftier than him. In fact, if you go to Nantes in France, you'll find he has a street named after him. They like a bit of craftiness, the French. And no one was more French than Terront, who satisfied all the old stereotypes of his countrymen as bad-tempered, vain, contrary and, of course, devious.

In November 1878 Terront rode the world's first six-day race, at the Agricultural Hall in Islington, north London, (the hall is still there, but it's called the Business Design Centre these days; take the Underground to Angel station if you want to find it and follow the signs from there) and charmed nobody by openly racing for money, demanding his prizes in cash, regarding his rivals with contempt and considering himself altogether superior.

The British, who still had notions of sport as a challenge between gentlemen and accepted money only "reluctantly", ganged up against him. They rode harder when Terront came on to the track. They chased after him when he put in an effort. They raced even faster when he left the track. And they arranged to have their food handed up as they rode, forcing Terront to go out into the street to find a restaurant.

At some time they suggested a truce. They brought him flowers which they insisted he sniff, he said. But Terront's elegant French nose spotted more than the perfume of flowers. It sniffed out a trick as well. The flowers had been sprinkled with sleeping powder, he claimed, and from then on he wouldn't accept anything from anyone. His café trips became not simply time-wasting but essential. And every time he made them, of course, the others lowered their heads to the handlebars and went as fast as they could.

The world's first six-day race wasn't a happy experience for him. He felt cheated and despised. He felt sick on the tight unbanked track that ran round a hall normally used for cattle shows. He felt, rightly, that the British despised him. And he went home to Paris with just £10 (about $15 but worth a lot more then) for coming fifth. The winner, with 260 km, was an Englishman called Bill Cann.

Maybe that was what made him ride from then on with both his head and his legs. It was all very well being France's big star of long-distance racing, but that was no good if he couldn't think his way out of a fix.

The big sign that he had learned to both think and race came in February 1893, when a promoter in Paris engaged him to ride an extraordinary 1,000 km race against Valentin Corre of Brittany, his big rival who'd come third in Bordeaux–Paris. The race was to be held in the city centre, at the Galérie des Machines, and things went wrong from the start. As if the distance wasn't enough, the people who ran Paris made things harder by refusing to keep the lights on all night. Faced with a disaster before the event had even started, the organisers were forced to borrow generators and lamps from workmen who were building a hangar near the Eiffel Tower.

That kept the track lit but when Paris said there would be no light they should have added that there'd be no heating either. This was February, remember. The organisers had to go back to the builders and borrow braziers to warm the spectators. But if you've ever seen strikers huddling around their makeshift fires outside factories, you'll know that braziers don't throw their heat very far. Those who got near them were as happy as they were likely to be on a cold winter night but the rest were still freezing. It didn't take them long to find a solution: they ripped out 600 wooden seats from the stands, heaped them high, set fire to them and crowded happily round the bonfire.

Down on the track, Terront and Corre eyed each other nervously. Each was surrounded by a team of helpers, including relays of pacers who would set up the speed for them and provide a slipstream. That was considered not only normal but desirable in those days, because what people wanted was to see riders going as fast as they could.

There's not much to say about the race. It was, after all, just two men going round and round and round. Spectators sensed the boredom they were in for and only the committed bought tickets. The stadium, with its smoking remains of wooden seats, was half empty. But then things took an unusual twist.

A 1,000 km race takes a long time. To be exact, this one took 41 hours and 2,500 laps. It also takes a lot of liquid. Both men had to deal, as the French newspapers expressed it, with their biological needs. Each also refused to give in until he'd seen the other climb off his bike and disappear into his trackside cabin.

Well, Corre watched and watched. The laps built up, the hours passed and the bottles of drink were emptied. But not once in 27 hours did Terront budge from his saddle. Not once did he show even a hint of distress. Corre looked on with growing despair and finally he could stand it no more. He called for his pacers to stop, steered painfully into the track centre, and felt the relief that only a man who hasn't relieved himself for 27 hours can possibly feel.

Terront, meanwhile, cruised on unaffected. This was clearly a giant among men. Or at least a giant among bladders.

The relief took Corre several minutes and he was six laps down by the time he started racing again. The track was later rebuilt at 333 m and with bankings but in those days it was 400 m, so he had lost close to two and a half kilometers. More than that, he was mentally and physically broken. He managed only a few hours next time before he stopped, once more losing time as Terront rode on unperturbed. And still he couldn't work out how Terront could do it.

Next morning he found out. Some of his helpers had left the track at dawn to fetch more food and there they bought a paper. What they had missed from their position inside the track, the reporters sitting in the outside seats had spotted. The headline that caught the helpers' eyes was *Le coup de la chambre à air.* A *coup* means what it does in *coup d'état* or *coup de grace*; a *chambre à air* in French is an inner tube.

Aghast, the helpers felt a cold chill run through them as they read the closely spaced black type that unveiled Terront's ruse. Far from enjoying a superhuman bladder, he had simply cut half a meter from an inner tube, knotted one end and given it to his pacers. Every so often he had crowded his assistants around him, taken the knotted inner tube, pushed it down his shorts and filled it as he rode. It was as difficult as it was clever; cycling shorts were much looser in those days but Terront had no freewheel and he had to keep pedalling. When the job was done, Corre's helpers read in horror, Terront had merely retrieved the tube from his shorts and handed it back to a pacer. The assistant then rode off the track, emptied the tube and kept it for next time.

If Corre's team were impressed, it was nothing compared to the reaction of the people of Paris. The trick was the sensation of a cold winter's day, and people who until then had had no interest in a boring bike race now wanted to see Terront use his inner tube. They wanted to see what Corre could come up with in revenge. They were so keen that crowds formed all down the street.

The more the crowds formed, the more other people worried they were missing out on something. They began offering the organisers more than the five-franc value of the ticket so they could jump the queue. The promoters, who'd had enough of all the troubles they'd been through, found manna dropping from heaven all round them. This wasn't a chance to be missed and they sold tickets for far more than the hall could hold. The flimsy upper balconies began filling ten deep and people started sitting in the rafters. Word got out and the police arrived and demanded they come down. But people in rafters are in a secure position so far as raids by the police are concerned and the more the gendarmes demanded they come down, the more they yelled insults from the safety of the roof. Meanwhile the promoters counted their cash.

The 1,000 km passed in 41:50:04, with Corre 9.3 km behind Terront. The crowd that the police hadn't managed to evict came down on to the track to carry Terront in triumph. Corre, meanwhile, sat on his trackside bed exhausted and largely neglected.

"Terront didn't even beat me by a tire," he told journalists slowly with a wry smile. "He won by an inner tube."

Terront became a huge celebrity, France's first bike hero, the first André Leducq ("a rider who was liked by women, whom he honoured as frequently as his track contracts," a friend recalled), Jacques Anquetil, Bernard Hinault or Laurent Jalabert.

Remember him if you ever ride Paris–Brest–Paris. Terront won it in 1891, when the roads were bumpy mud and cobbles were considered a luxury. He finished the 1,198 km in 71½ hours. Today, on smooth roads, on modern bikes with multiple gears and good lights, riding in huge groups, riders more than a century later consider themselves satisfied if they get round within 20 hours of that time.

2

HOW TO MAKE FRIENDS...

Since we've started on a fairly base tone, let's stay on it for a moment...

One of the best bits of being a professional is to be paid to go away to the sun to train in the winter. Amateurs have to stay at home and shiver in the sleet and rain while their betters are paid to ride in Italy and the south of France, or more and more these days, to race in Australia and the Middle East. In fact professionals have been going to training camps since the days of Norbert Peugeot in 1908. He wanted his team to have the edge over the Alcyon team, its big rival in its kingfisher-blue jerseys. So Norbert pulled out his cheque book and sent his riders to train in the south of France.

The idea didn't catch on, the riders being more impressed than Alcyon, who laughed at Peugeot for wasting his money and pampering men employed to suffer like mules. Not until the 1950s did the camps start again. By then the best riders had their own private cars and no longer had to ride to races or go by train. And teams which often paid their riders nothing more than their everyday expenses began to have enough spare cash to cover a week or so in a hotel.

But how seriously do professionals take these sessions? Are they serious stints of grinding out the miles and wearing away the fat? Or is there—as you'd imagine there would be with a bunch of young men away from home together—a less serious side? That was the question that the young American, Justin Spinelli, asked himself when he joined Mario Cipollini's training camp in 2001. This was a boy who took up cycling when he was 15 "because it looked pretty cool", then found himself dumped by the Dutch team he'd joined and his contract with Cipo's team mysteriously cut from two years to one. He went to the training camp nervously, then, anxious to make an impression, desperate not to say or do the wrong thing, eager to show he could be one of the lads in a team where he didn't speak the language. But if he suspected highjinks, he could never have guessed the initiation ceremony that awaited him.

The camp had barely started when his team-mates grabbed him, held him down and forced him to watch as another team-mate exposed his backside. Then the unfortunate American was blindfolded and someone pushed a slimy finger into his mouth. When the wrap was removed, Spinelli looked down to see the finger and that he had been sucking a very lavatorial brown filth. There was only one conclusion and he grew predictably angry. How could his so-called friends do such a thing? Worse, how could they do it and then fall about laughing? He didn't know whether to flee the room, be sick or just cry. The more distressed he looked, the more the others roared. Finally, they revealed the mixture was nothing more than chocolate spread and massage cream.

Cipollini, the team's flamboyant leader, insisted it was all part of bringing his team together, especially those who weren't Italian. The laughs over, he had his team out on to the road at 9:30 the next morning. They were probably still laughing and joking about the fun they'd had with Spinelli. But not for long. Their next training session was 177 km long and climbed 3,000 m. With more again the next day, and the day after that.

Compared to that, a lavatorial finger could even seem attractive. But then again, disillusioned by being not so much a "cool" professional racing cyclist as "a pawn in some marketing man's strategic game", maybe it summarises the way life can be in a hard sport where little more than results—and sales—count.

3

HOW TO WIN WITHOUT TRYING

All round France, in market places, on the walls of post offices and anywhere else the French care to put them, you can find enamelled metal plates about the size of a tabloid newspaper. They display the words that Charles de Gaulle broadcast to the French from the BBC in London, the speech about France having lost a battle but not a war.

De Gaulle was an unmissable man, not only for his size and his trumpet-like nose (down which he gazed in dismay at the rest of the world as though it could never rise to his heights) but because his voice boomed with import-laden French which commanded attention. Which made it all the more surprising that in 1960 the unknown Frenchman, Pierre Beuffeuil, should have missed him while passing through his village. It was a happy mistake and it won Beuffeuil a rare moment of glory, for on Saturday July 16, 1960 his oversight won him a stage of the Tour de France.

That day, Charles de Gaulle was in the village of Colombey-les-Deux-Églises, east of Troyes, where he and his wife had their private house. There Madame de Gaulle—known across France as Tante Yvonne (Aunt Yvonne) for her impressive dowdiness—quietly read books or embroidered while her husband relaxed with his records of military marches. The Tour was due to pass through their village in a stage from Besançon to Troyes and the president let the organisers know he would be at the foot of his garden to watch.

Such news was not to be taken lightly in France. De Gaulle was the closest the nation had had to a king since Louis XVI, as close to an emperor since Napoléon. News that he would be in his garden was more than just a strong hint, and the organiser, Jacques Goddet, took it. He approached Henry Anglade, the national champion, who recalled: "We were right at the end of the Tour, the day before we finished in

Paris. I was at the back of the bunch when Jacques Goddet came up alongside me. He said 'We've just learned that General de Gaulle is at Colombey. Would it be an inconvenience if the race stopped to greet him?' I said to him, 'You're asking all the riders to stop in full flight…'"

Goddet looked at Anglade again, realised he was indeed asking to stop the race in full flight, and then sent a motorcyclist ahead to confirm that de Gaulle was there. It'd be embarrassing to squeal to a halt and find the president had gone for a walk elsewhere. In time the motorcyclist came back and said that indeed de Gaulle was at Colombey, standing in the street at the end of his garden like the most humble spectator in the world, surrounded by men in shirtsleeves and women in aprons.

Anglade recalled: "I went back up to the head of the race to talk to the team leaders, and then I dropped back down the bunch telling the other riders as they passed. Finally I dropped back to the race director's car to say that the riders had all agreed."

The race rolled into Colombey-les-Deux-Églises and started to brake. Goddet, ahead of the race, pulled up alongside the French president, an admiral, and the president's minder Roger Tessier (who was 20 cm shorter than the man he was supposed to protect). Then he looked considerably upwards to meet de Gaulle's gaze and said: "Monsieur le Président, the Tour de France has stopped at Colombey to salute you." To which de Gaulle, to whom such a preposterous idea had naturally never occurred, said: "*Monsieur le Directeur, il ne fallait pas*"—"It really wasn't necessary."

De Gaulle spotted Anglade's French championship jersey and told him he knew all about him. Then he saw the *maillot jaune* of Italy's Gastone Nencini, whom he said he recognised from television. And then he walked round the bunch shaking hands. It was a great honour. But not as great for some as it was to others.

For a start, a handful of Belgian riders grew confused and thought a strike had started. Many Belgians don't speak good French, or can't be bothered to, but a strike is a strike and it was probably in a good cause and so they were happy to join in. They didn't know what it was about but there was time to have a pee before they took the trouble to find out, so while de Gaulle was shaking hands on one side of the group, the Belgians began watering the road on the other. A group of similarly puzzled Spaniards, who were smaller than the rest and couldn't see over everyone else's heads to see what was going on, began a noisy argument over some dispute which had broken out earlier in the day.

The other man who knew nothing of the stop was Pierre Beuffeuil. Anglade's message had never reached him. He wasn't in the bunch at the crucial time because he'd had a puncture and he was still chasing back to the race. He was too minor a rider for his team-mates to bother to stop and help and so he was destined to a long, hard race back to the bunch. It wasn't a chase he was enjoying. The riders, after all, were in "full flight" as Anglade put it. And then the impossible appeared in front of his eyes. The whole race had halted by the roadside. The Belgians may have thought it was a strike, the Spaniards could still be bickering and the French may have been keen to greet their president, but Beuffeuil was in no mind to join any of them. He cashed in on the two-minute stop and put his head down and raced on to Troyes. There he won the stage, one of only two in his career, and he has dined out on the story ever since.

If you wonder, by the way, why General de Gaulle had an admiral at the foot of his garden that day, all I can say is that that was the kind of man he was.

4

HOW TO HAVE THE WRONG NAME

Many riders have competed under false names. Among the competitors in the first long road race, Paris–Rouen in November 1869, was a hefty British woman calling herself Miss America. Among the aggravations she had to face as well as the distance, the awful roads and the lack of experience, was being chased out of villages by lusty men shouting rude suggestions. Another competitor styled himself Peter the First. It is unlikely that he was similarly chased.

The winner of the 1904 Tour de France, shown in the record books as Henri Cornet, was actually called Henri Jaudry. If there was a good reason why he changed his name, I don't know it.

Some riders changed their name because of a misunderstanding, like Lucien Petit-Breton, who declined to give his surname of Mazan to a race clerk because he didn't want his family to discover he was entering bike races. His father had banned him from wasting time with ruffians in cycling clubs. Instead he blurted: "I'm a Breton", meaning he was from Brittany. The clerk already had a Breton in his list, and a taller one at that, and so he entered Mazan as Petit-Breton. The name stuck. It didn't stop him winning the Tour in 1907 and 1908.

Others, like Miss America, just fancied a more striking name. A Belgian rider called Julien Lootens, for instance, rode the 1903 Tour as Samson and finished sixth, winning 700 francs. Much later, Edouard Stablewski became Jean Stablinski, the 1962 world champion, because French journalists covering the Peace Race repeatedly got his name wrong. In the end he decided it was easier to call himself Jean Stablinski and be done with it.

Odder are the families which realise they've made a mistake. The multiple winner of Paris–Nice, the Irish rider Sean Kelly, isn't called Sean at all. His real name is John Kelly. His biographer, David Walsh, says: "The new baby was christened John James, after his father. But, in the great tradition of Irish curiosities, his name was immediately changed to Sean so that he would not be confused with his dad, the real John James Kelly. Now neither version is known by the names which appear on their birth certificates. The senior one is called Jack and the son Sean."

Sean is the translation of John in the ancient Irish language. Jack is just the kind of name men get when they hang about with farming folk.

But that's nothing compared to Servais Knaven, the Dutchman of whom nobody had heard until he won Paris–Roubaix in 2001. Journalists were too occupied with finding out who he was and how he'd won against much more illustrious opposition to wonder whether his name really was Servais Knaven. Had they asked—and to be fair, it's an improbable question—they'd have found that he was actually called Hendrikus, or Rik or Hennie for short.

So why is the 2001 Paris–Roubaix listed as being won by a man who doesn't exist? Why is he known by the wrong name? How did it happen? In Servais'—or Hendrikus'—own words: "So far as I know, my father was so delighted to have a son that he'd emptied several beers too many when he went to the town hall to register my birth. He forgot that my first name was going to be Servais and he only wrote Hendrikus [his intended second name]. He went back to the office a little bit later but they insisted that he pay 200 guilders to change my name. That was a lot of money at the time for my parents, so officially my name stayed as Hendrikus but I've always been called Servais."

5

HOW TO RIDE AN INTERNATIONAL TIME TRIAL

The place I had to go was Hazelaarstraat in the village of St-Willebrord. You can find it in southern Holland, almost as far south as you can get, down by the Belgian border. I rode into the village as it was getting dark and, not knowing the way, I stopped to ask some builders working by lamplight. They were glad of the rest and to oblige a foreigner.

"*De Hazelaarstraat wilt-ie, jongens,*" one asked his pals for guidance. Everybody downed spades and leaned against a concrete mixer for a conference in wellingtons and heavy dialect.

"That's where van Est lives, isn't it?" one of them said after a while.

"*Precies,*" I said.

They laughed.

"Why didn't you say so in the first place, then?" they asked. "Everyone knows where van Est lives."

He was waiting for me when I got there, as barrel-shaped as when he was racing but dressed now in old trousers, cardigan and slippers. He laughed, he drank, he smoked (without inhaling, he said), he watched soccer as we talked, he banged on the table in amusement at the absurdity of his own life, and he grabbed my arm as he started on yet another anecdote. Yes, Wim van Est was a man who thought the world was great fun.

This was the man who was the first Dutchman to win the *maillot jaune*, the first Dutchman to wear the pink jersey of the Giro, the first to win the Tour of Flanders. He won Bordeaux–Paris three times.

What he never won was the Grand Prix des Nations. For a quarter of a century, the Nations was the world's unofficial time-trial championship. It started near the château of Versailles and followed a triangle through Rambouillet, Maulette, St-Rémy-les-Chevreuse, Versailles and Boulogne to finish originally on the Buffalo track in Paris where Henri Desgrange, the founder of the Tour de France, set the world's first ratified hour record in 1893.

There were three hills, one in the first 100 km, lots of cobbles, and the last 40 km went through the woods of the Vallée de Chevreuse, a popular area for bike riders. It was 142 km long. The first was in 1932 but not until Fausto Coppi won in 1946 and 1947 did it gain its real glamour. By then van Est was the one big name on the road in Holland and the organisers wanted him to make their event still more international.

"I was the first real star that we had in Holland," van Est said with not a trace of pomposity or bragging. "On the road, anyway. I mean, we had Gerrit Schulte, Kees Pellenaars, van Vliet and Derksen on the track, but…

"Anyway, in 1949 I got a contract to ride the Grand Prix des Nations, because I'd won a time-trial in the Tour of Holland, in front of Koblet and good time-triallists, and good Belgians. And I could have won that, too, but I went wrong. I'd never been to France. And I went on the train to Paris, and you had to take a *carnet*, a little book, for the bike, for the Customs. Everything, spare wheels, everything had to be in the book. And I didn't understand a word of French. *Niks!*

"And there was this Frenchman, great big moustache, and he was talking French and I was speaking Dutch and, ja, he was saying '*Parlez français!*' and I was shaking my head, '*Non! Non!*' and he couldn't explain and I couldn't understand and, anyway, eventually I got away after an hour.

"And so then I had to get to a hotel. All I had was a card from the manager: boulevard Magenta, Hotel d'Angleterre, near the Gare de Nord station. I thought, 'I'll take a taxi.' And there was this other Frenchman saying '*Pas bicyclette! Pas bicyclette!*' and I was saying, '*Ja, bicyclette! Ja, bicyclette!*' and we got it all taken to bits and I shoved it up front with the meter, and we were driving and driving. Eiffel Tower, Place Pigalle, Place de Napoléon, the Sacré Coeur … and then the Eiffel Tower again.

“I said, ‘We’ve already been by here! *Allez hôtel! Allez hôtel!*’ And he was saying, ‘*Piano! Piano! Doucement!*’ And by then I was getting really angry, and I was banging on the window and shouting ‘*Godverdomme, hotel!*’ I was in that taxi for an hour and a half, *godverdomme*.

“And then when I got there, there was this hotel man, the *garçon*, with a moustache and a blue apron, and I took the bike upstairs to my room. I mean, it was no chic hotel—just bare floors and old furniture. Well! By five o’clock the cleaning lady was complaining to the *patron* because the bike was dirty, because the previous day I’d won a race in Belgium and it’d been raining all day.

“My leather saddle was soaked, my shoes were wet through, and so he said, the *patron*, ‘Let’s take them down to the boiler room, away from the room.’ And that was fine. But next morning—the race was in the afternoon—I thought I’d go out training. There was nothing happening in Paris, no cars, nothing, before 11 AM. So I put on my tracksuit and everything and I went down to the boiler room. And I just about fell over with shock.

“He’d put my shoes on the top of the stove and leaned my bike against it as well. And, *verdorie*, the saddle was about 10 cm long. Dried up. All crumpled up from drying out. And my shoes would have fitted a five-year-old. I didn’t dare race. I thought I’d have to go back to the station.”

Wondering what to do next, van Est wandered into the street. And there, by chance, he met a group of Belgian reporters out for a stroll. People who live as far south in Holland as van Est did consider themselves more Belgian than Dutch and so there was an instant rapport. Delighted to be able to help, and to have such a wonderful story to report, they searched Paris for a bike shop prepared to lend van Est a bike and shoes. It seemed an easy task at first but the best they could find him was a pair of second-hand shoes and a bike with one brake. And with those van Est rode his first Grand Prix des Nations, the unofficial world championship.

The story, of course, doesn’t end there. With van Est you’d expect nothing else. Despite all that had happened he finished second by 13 seconds … after being misdirected at the entrance to the track at the Parc des Princes. The winner was the Frenchman, Charles Coste.

"*Oh jongen,*" van Est said with another huge laugh and a thump on the table, "those were unbelievable times."

Rest assured: he will return to our story. But, sadly, he won't return in person. He died in May 2003. He was 80, one of 16 brothers and sisters. One of the warmest and happiest characters had left the sport. He'll always be remembered in St-Willebrord, though; the mayor changed the rules about naming a street after a living person and in his last years Wim van Est had the quiet satisfaction of walking down his own road.

6

HOW TO MAKE ... and lose ... YOUR MONEY

Many bike riders have been bad with money. Freddy Maertens lost most of his through bad investments. So did Michel Pollentier. Others have been good at hanging on to it. Rik van Steenbergen, for instance, once turned up for an engagement at Herne Hill track in London and demanded his appearance money before he'd go into even the changing rooms. The organiser had to raid the ticket office tills and even empty his own wallet. The French writer René de Latour said van Steenbergen liked to play the stock market with friends who gave him tips in return for tickets to vélodromes. But, de Latour added, they were often tickets that van Steenbergen had received for nothing in the first place.

I made a few calls and came across a colleague who, years back, was trying to make a name for himself in Belgium so that he could turn professional. He never did it but he did ride the supporting amateur races at Belgian six-days, where he could see van Steenbergen close up.

"Every time there was a gap in the program," the man told me, "you could see van Steenbergen walk into the bar like a big shambling bear. Other riders used to relax in their cabins or have a massage down in the riders' area downstairs. But not van Steenbergen. He would go into the bar in his race clothes, maybe with a tracksuit on, and start playing cards.

"When the time came to start racing again, he'd say good-bye to the group he'd been playing with, leave behind the money he'd lost or scoop up what he'd won, and wander back into the track. The funny thing is that it never seemed to bother him whether he won or lost and sometimes I wonder if he even knew. It was just the chance to sit in a bar and play cards that appealed to him. You'd think the card games were more important than the bike races, and maybe he'd ridden so many races by then that perhaps they were. I've never known a rider like him."

When it came to being easy with both his own money and that of others, though, few can match the 24-year-old Frenchman Louis "Trou-Trou" Trousselier. In 1905 he was in the army, in the 101st Regiment where he was a conscript. That summer he asked for a few days' leave "to do some cycling" and was given them. The "some cycling" turned out to be the Tour de France.

Relieved of his army boots and uniform, Trou-Trou—the nickname means "hole" but it's no more than a play on his name—won five stages against the three stage wins of each of the other big names, Hippolyte Aucouturier and Jean-Baptiste Dortignacq. That year's Tour was on points rather than time because the organiser, Henri Desgrange, didn't want to penalise riders forced to repair their own bikes. In those days riders were separated on the road by hours so a repair would cost a rider a lot of time but not necessarily change his position. By contrast, penalising a rider for a lengthy repair seemed unfair.

Having won so many stages and been so well placed in others, Trousselier was unbeatable by Bordeaux. He was so far ahead on points that no one could pass him. That, of course, pleased him. But it gave him extra pleasure, too, because he'd told his officers back in the barracks that he'd be away for only a day. The only way he could avoid being jailed for deserting was to get back and tell them he had brought the army glory by winning the Tour de France.

Things might have worked out better had he actually done that, had he gone straight home. But winning the Tour made him realise there was more to life than soldiering. He had enough money that the sergeant could wait a little longer. He would have a night out in Paris instead. The money that gave him confidence was a fortune. He had won 6,950 francs in prizes, including 4,000 for winning. He got a bonus from Peugeot, which made his bike. And because contracts were already coming in for the races he would ride after Paris, he had

25,000 francs. That would be worth $6,000 these days, which doesn't sound a lot. But in 1905 it represented almost 50 years' wages.

It's from this point on that facing the wrath of the army should have seemed a better option. Instead, he had a night at one of Paris's bike tracks, enjoying himself with other riders. The announcer there, Georges Berretrot, remembered: "He shut himself away in one of the cabins at the Buffalo track with two colleagues. They sat round a massage table and the dice rolled all night and much of the following morning. By the time Trousselier left the cabin, he didn't have a coin in his pocket. He'd lost everything he'd suffered to win on the road. He'd had the joy of winning the Tour de France and he'd been delighted to win. And to his credit, he accepted his losses without a grumble and had only one thought—to get back on his bike and win some money all over again."

Sadly, his career was never the same again. He came third in the next year's Tour and won Bordeaux–Paris in 1908 but that was about it.

If Trousselier was careless with his own money, he showed the same easygoing attitude to other people's as well. For Trousselier was the master of the Free Meal Trick. It would still work today but you, of course, are too honest to try ...

What he would do was go out riding with two or three friends. They would enjoy themselves all morning and then head for the nearest town soon after noon. And there they would look for the most expensive restaurant and go inside. The head waiter would welcome them, they would sit at their table and then they would order the most expensive meal on the menu. For a while they would talk quietly as they ate, but then they would start arguing, getting heated, until in the end other customers were disturbed and the *patron* would come over to ask if all was well.

Trousselier would apologise and explain the argument. They couldn't agree which of them was the best rider. One would list the races he had won, others would claim to be better sprinters or climbers, and so it would go on. Perhaps, Trousselier suggested, the *patron* could help settle the dispute. Would he suggest a landmark a kilometer or so down the road and set them off in a race there and back?

The *patron* would get a free bike race, the other diners would be entertained, and the losers would pay for the meal. Time and again the *patron* would agree … and time and again the riders would disappear down the road and leave the unpaid bill behind them.

7

HOW TO RIDE THE TOUR DE FRANCE IN STYLE

In the spring of 1907, the Baron Henri Pépin de Gontaud—a classy name, you have to admit—had a remarkable idea. He called his valets into the grandest room of his château outside Toulouse and announced that they were to ride the Tour de France with him. And not just ride it, 350 km stages and all, but pace their rich master around the country at the speed he cared to ride and, when necessary, mend his tires and clean his bike.

The valets, you assume, were astonished. Until then their job had been to polish the cutlery, iron the baron's shirts, sort his underwear and answer the door to callers. Riding this new Tour de France, the world's longest race, hadn't been in their deal when they signed on. The baron knew all that, of course, but he promised them that in return for their efforts, they would stay at the best hotels and dine at the finest restaurants. He had no intention of winning, he said. Indeed, if they went too fast they would have no time to live well as they circuited France. But whether they won or not, he would pay each of them the 4,000 francs the winner would receive and they would all return to the château when they had had enough.

And so on July 8 Henri joined the peloton of 112 at the Porte Bineau, along with Jean Dargassies and Henri Gauban, having taken the train to Paris. Pépin was rider number 59 and the only one in the field, other than his valets, who had absolutely no intention of winning the Tour de France, still less mixing it with sweaty, muscular ruffians like Gustave Garrigou, Émile Georget and Lucien Petit-Breton, the favourites. And so while the stars fiddled with their bikes and took last-minute advice from their helpers, he spent his time lifting his boater to the ladies and blowing them kisses.

The race started at 5:30 AM but still the aristocrat and his men were in no hurry. Pépin finished his conversation with a lady and only then turned to his valets and said: "Let us depart. But remember—we have all the time in the world." By then the bunch had already disappeared on its eight-hour journey north to Roubaix.

The three buccaneers never separated. Next day they took 12 hours 20 minutes longer than Émile Georget on the stage from Roubaix to Metz and the judges were furious. The race was on points rather than time so, since when riders got in mattered less than the order in which they arrived, the judges had to wait for everyone. It was only after that that Henri Desgrange, the organiser, decided on the time limits that we still know today.

One day the trio was astonished to come across another rider. Usually the rest of the race was too far ahead and they saw other competitors only at the start. This man wasn't riding, it's true, because he was lying in a ditch and groaning. But it was such a novelty to see someone else that they peered down to see who it could be.

"My name is Jean-Marie Teychenne," the miserable figure said. "Like you, I am a racer. But I have the most terrible *fringale* [hunger]. Leave me, I'm done for."

Pépin recognised the man's accent as from Toulouse, which is where the baron had his château. And while the count certainly didn't speak with anything as common as the local accent, he recognised a fellow Toulousain, a man who said *veng* for *vin* and Toulous-*uh* for Toulouse. He ordered Dargassies and Gauban to pull him out.

"And now you will join us," Pépin announced grandly, slapping him on the back and telling his helpers to wipe the mud off his number 76. "We are but three but we live well and we shall finish this race. We may not win, but we shall see France and see it in style." And so they set off, now a foursome, with the bewildered Teychenne cleaned and fed at the next inn and feeling altogether better.

And did they finish? Well, no. Somewhere between Lyon and Grenoble on stage five, Pépin decided he'd had a lovely time, paid out the money he'd promised his helpers and set off for the train home. And so ended one of the most colourful stories of Tour history.

The nice thing is that it's true. Sure enough the tale has grown in the telling, but there was an Henri Pépin and there were two hired riders and he certainly was rich enough not to trouble Henri Desgrange, the Tour organiser, for anything as common as money. I know that because I've seen the letter that Desgrange wrote to him on August 31, 1907, four weeks after the race ended. It said: "Dear Monsieur Pépin, it is with the greatest pleasure that, according to the desire you expressed in your last letter, instead of sending you cash for the allowances owed to you, *L'Auto* will provide you with a medal to the same value." It was signed with just the initials H.D., in exactly the way that they reappeared on the yellow jersey in 2003.

And it was "Monsieur Pépin", you notice, not "Monsieur le Baron." France had done away with barons a century earlier and Pépin wasn't even the descendant of a baron. In fact the aristocratic "de Gontaud" in his name was his address. He went to the Tour with a large trunk of belongings stencilled in gold script with his name and then, because he lived in the village of Gontaud-de-Nogaret—nearer to Bordeaux than Toulouse—the words "de Gontaud, Lot et Garonne" and the two were run together and Pépin was promoted to a noble.

There was no château, either. Henri lived in an anonymous grey house in the main street of Gontaud-de-Nogaret. In fact it's still there. The road these days is called the rue de Bantzenheim, after the village with which Gontaud is twinned, and Pépin's house is almost next to the ironmonger's. It's closed up these days and has been for a long time. I'm told it's in a poor state inside.

In his day, though, he lived there in some glory, rich enough never to have to work, what the French call a *propriétaire*. Far from being a dilettante, he was an established racer and record-breaker who got his pictures in magazines. Above my desk right now is the front cover of *Le Cycle* of October 28, 1894, which shows him riding a racing bike of the period in knee-length shorts and a long-sleeved jersey. He has tired eyes and a weak chin strengthened by the twizzled moustache that men adopted at the time. The bike has a sloping top tube, which shows that little is ever new in the world of bike design.

Dargassies and Gauban weren't valets but experienced riders. These days we'd call them domestiques, but neither the name nor the idea existed at the time. Dargassies was a blacksmith from Grisolles, north-west of Toulouse. He rode the first Tour in 1903 even though he'd bought his first bike only two months earlier. He'd never heard of the race and he went to Paris—a lifetime's journey—because the man in the bike shop said he looked strong enough to have a go. Géo Lefèvre, the race clerk and the man who thought up the idea of the Tour de France, tried to talk him out of riding, but Dargassies insisted that hard labour was nothing new to a man who worked with hammer and anvil and that he rode daily between Montauban and Grisolles.

Dargassies and Gauban also rode the 1905 race, Pépin's first, and it was probably there that they got to know each other. The pair's experience would be why they asked Pépin to compensate them for what they could have won on their own account.

And what happened to our baron? Well, he was born in 1864, on November 18, and always made a point of saying that it was six years before the painter, Toulouse-Lautrec, a fact that amused him for some reason. In 1914 he rode the Tour de France for the third time and that year died of "athleticism." I have no idea what "athleticism" meant but people in those days died of almost anything. He was only 50. He spent his last two years in the house at Gontaud with his chipped, grey shutters.

As for the others, Dargassies joined Pépin on the train. Gauban continued and got better and better, gaining almost two hours until by stage eight he was only 36 minutes in arrears. But something happened on stage nine and he dropped to 2 hours 12 minutes. Despite pulling back to an hour and six minutes on stage 10, where he finished 14th, he pulled out on the 11th. It was his fifth and final Tour.

It was also the last for Dargassies, who came 11th in 1903—his first race, remember—and fourth in 1904 before abandoning in 1905 and 1907.

And the man in the ditch? Well, Jean-Marie Teychenne came 81st on the first stage of 1907 and finished along with the others, although discreetly allowing Pépin to cross the line first. They were joint 65th or 81st (early Tour results split times to decimals of seconds but are notoriously inaccurate in everything else), four hours ten minutes down. There seems to be no record of him from then on. I doubt he got a share of Pépin's largesse but I like to think that he was grateful for the free meals.

8

HOW TO LOWER THE TONE

Henri Pépin, whether he was a baron or not, brought a certain class to cycling. That wasn't the view that people took of Edward Battel and Frank Keeping back in 1896.

Battel and Keeping were servants at the British embassy in Athens, which is where the Olympic Games happened to be. "Happened" because these were the first of the revived series and Greece was the Olympics' spiritual home. The idea of a global sports meeting wasn't as big then as it is now and the Olympics were small enough to accept anyone who wanted to take part. In fact some years back France decided to find all its surviving Olympic medallists and succeeded in locating all but one. Then researchers found an old man who seemed to remember that, yes, he had ridden some big race somewhere or other when he was young but it hadn't struck him as important.

"But it was the Olympic Games," the historians told him.

"Really?" said the old man. "I had no idea."

Battel and Keeping were in Athens when the Olympics were held and thought they, too, would have a go. They entered for the bike races. You'd think Britain would be proud of them, if only because they'd saved the nation having to pay their fares to Greece. But it was nothing of the sort. Their country's sports leaders objected that they weren't true amateurs. To be an amateur, to them, meant having a private income that made prizes from sport irrelevant. If you had enough money of your own, you had no need for prizes in races and so you were a true amateur untainted by cash. Battel and Keeping, though, were working men and very keen on cash, not to live well but merely to live. Their salaries at the embassy were just about enough to get by on but what little they earned meant they were "not gentlemen and so they could not possibly be amateurs"—and so they were ruled out of the Olympics.

The rest of the world had rather more sense and the two took part after Britain was told it was being stuffy and ridiculous. Battel rode the road race and came third, finishing bruised and bleeding after crashing on the rutted roads from Athens to Marathon and back. These days third place would have earned him a medal, but not then. Only the winner and his runner-up received anything, a silver medal and a crown of olives for the first and a bronze medal and an olive crown for the second. Had he not crashed, Battel might have won. Instead he was beaten by a local rider, Aristidis Konstantinides, who had also crashed, wrecked his bike, borrowed another, swerved in the streets of Athens to avoid a spectator and run into a wall. After all that, he probably deserved to win.

As for Keeping, he had misery of his own. He elected to ride the 12-hour race on the track, where he finished with 899 laps to the 900 of Austria's Adolf Schmal. The race started at 5 AM with just six riders, four of them Greek, and few people turned out to watch in the cold, wet weather because, say reports, "it was a monotonous sight."

The spectacle they missed was of Keeping and Schmal growing more and more wretched until both could barely continue riding. Richard D. Mandell, in *The First Modern Olympics*, says: "Neither had eaten and had only sipped liquid. They were squalid from excreta and delirious from fatigue … their legs swollen gruesomely … both could be heard weeping."

That was when bike races were for real men and not the pampered wimps of nowadays…

9

HOW TO ALMOST BREAK A RECORD

Dick Poole could probably be heard weeping, too. Or at least groaning in black despair. Because Dick Poole is the Englishman who thought he'd broken Britain's longest record—and then found he hadn't. By about as far as you could bowl a wheel.

The British have always been intrigued by Land's End, in the bottom south-west of their country, and the quaintly named John o'Groats in the very north of Scotland. The route between them is the longest distance you can travel on the British mainland. It works out at about 870 miles, the exact distance being up to the rider because he can take any route he likes provided he starts and finishes in the right places.

The first record was set by George Mills, the winner of the first Bordeaux–Paris. He rode what the British still call a penny-farthing, a bike with a huge front wheel and a tiny trailing one that resembled the largest and smallest coins of the period. He finished in 5 days 1 hour 45 minutes. It was July 1886 and even now nobody has ridden a penny-farthing faster.

The first man in less than three days was Tom Peck in 1908. He took 2 days 22 hours 42 minutes despite two crashes in the Scottish Highlands. It took almost another 60 years for the record to fall to less than two days. Until, in fact, Richard William Ewart Poole, an accountant with a car company west of London during the week and a strictly amateur cyclist at weekends, set off at 9:45 AM on Wednesday, June 16, 1965 and reached John o'Groats in 1:23:46:35.

The ride was a spartan experience. Enthusiasts turned out in the middle of the night to stamp on the rubber pads set in the road in front of traffic lights to turn them green. These days lights have detectors under the road surface and change colour as traffic approaches, but stamping on the rubber was the only way in those days because a cyclist wasn't always heavy enough to set off the sensors himself.

None of the helpers was allowed to pass him on the road. They had to find complicated routes through country lanes to get round him, driving fast and with sleep-starved eyes along winding and unlit roads. Why? To make sure Poole got no help from the suction of a passing car. The rules were as spartan as the conditions.

Poole raced on through the rain. His battery lights refused to stay alight, his woolen clothing became sodden. Effective waterproofs and truly warm clothing had yet to be invented. There were no modern energy foods, either. Poole got through five liters of rice and fruit salad, three liters of a protein drink, 12 oranges, four liters of coffee, five liters of tea and four liters of a sticky, sugary drink called Ribena. He used two racing jerseys, two pairs of shorts, two pairs of shoes and several pairs of socks.

"I was in the state you'd expect after riding from one end of the country to the other," he said. "But they started saying I should go for the 1,000 miles record, the longest one there is. I didn't want to but they were saying it was only another 120 miles and I'd barely have to do it at touring speed. So I agreed and I had a rest and I set off again."

It was the 1,000 miles where things went wrong, although nobody realised it at the time. Poole's helpers calculated that he had 120 miles to go and that he'd need to ride at just 12 mph. And he did it easily. He rested for 30 minutes, set off at 20 mph for 45 minutes, then struggled on through hail and wind. The organiser, a semi-professional photographer called Bernard Thompson, followed in his van, driving the timekeeper and noting landmarks every mile and the time at which Poole passed them. They let him ride not just 1,000 miles but 1,010, just to be sure. Then they called him to a halt after two days eight minutes of almost non-stop riding. He had beaten the record by more than two and a half hours.

They didn't know where the 1,000 miles had passed, of course, but the route would have to be measured anyway and the exact finish and the time calculated. And so the measuring started. And it came out about 250 meters too short. Even with the extra 10 miles, it was just

250 meters short of the required 1,615,000. Poole *would* have broken the record had he ridden 1,000 miles—but the truth was that he hadn't. He had ridden 999.9.

"We couldn't understand it," he said. "They measured it again and then the motoring organisations joined in and they measured it and still it came out short. And it was getting to be quite a story in the papers. It took a lot of puzzling to work out what had happened. We had based our attempt on the schedule that Reg Randall, the previous holder, had used in 1960. The route was clear except in Scotland, where there was a choice between going straight over a mountain, which was the shorter route, or round it, which was longer but meant he could ride faster.

"We didn't know which way he'd gone and we couldn't tell from the route sheet because it didn't have distances, but we assumed the shorter way and that's the way I went. Unfortunately the over-the-mountain route was 10 miles and so many yards shorter and so I hadn't even done 1,000 miles when we were all sure that I'd ridden 1,010."

Poole never tried the record again. In his mind, he was the moral winner even though he never completed the distance. It was to take more than three decades before it actually fell. And then, at 10 AM on September 27, 2001, Gethin Butler set out to complete 1,000 miles—a complete 1,000 miles—in 2:07:53:07. Poole probably felt glad rather than sad that it had finally fallen.

10

HOW TO BE A MOUNTAIN KING

Of all the classics to win, the most glorious must be Milan–San Remo. The crowds are thick and passionate, the sun shines from an Italian sky, and little ranks higher in the Ferrari-and-sunglasses league of international glamour. What other race starts in a city of international sophistication and ends at one of the Mediterranean's most snooty resorts? It may mean more in muscular terms to win the Tour of Flanders or Paris–Roubaix, but …

The trouble is that Milan–San Remo is not always glamorous, not always warm. Take the case of the ever-unfortunate Eugène Christophe. You'll already know that Christophe was the first official *maillot jaune* in the Tour de France, and that he had to weld his forks back together at the foot of the Tourmalet because the rules wouldn't allow him a spare bike. But things like that seem dated because they could never happen again. On the other hand, what happened to him in Milan–San Remo in March 1910 is something we can all imagine. The next time you're on your bike on a bitterly cold day, shivering because you're mending a puncture and feeling sorry for yourself, remember Christophe, the guy with the moustache from the Malakoff area of Paris.

But let him tell the story in his own words …

"It was the second time I'd been to Milan," he recalled, "and I only knew a few words of the language. With Gustave Garrigou, I went to look at the course as far as Pavia, which was 30 kilometers. That was all I knew of the 290 kilometers of the race. I took Garrigou's advice, because he'd ridden before, in deciding which gears to use on the bikes I'd use before and after the Turchino climb.

"The weather had been good at the start of the week but it turned really bad and Alphonse Baugé [the manager] told us that we'd be going over the Turchino even though the road was bad and covered with snow. Everybody was talking about it and we began wondering if the race would be postponed. François Faber and Louis Trousselier cheered us up by saying 'What does it matter if we've got Lapize and Christophe, the two cyclo-cross champions, with us?'

"On Sunday morning April 3, 71 riders of the 94 who'd entered were set off in a biting cold. The roads were muddy and frozen and we had to bounce along in the ruts, riding on the verges between the posts that were spaced every 20 meters as far as Pavia. We rode the first 32 km in 56 minutes, the 53 km from Milan to Voghera in 1 hour 50. There were attacks after attack and it was more like a *course des primes* than a long-distance race …

"We got to the notorious Turchino. The clouds were low, the countryside was unattractive and we started to feel the cold more and more. We started to shiver and every turn of the pedals was heavier. The half-melted snow made the race very hard and we were struggling too with a glacial wind. I dropped my friend Ernest Paul to get up to Ganna, whom I could see on the hairpins. I got up and past him without too much trouble because he didn't seem to be withstanding the cold any better than I was.

"Not far from the summit I had to get off my bike because I started feeling bad. My fingers were rigid, my feet numb, my legs stiff and I was shaking continuously. I began walking and running to get my circulation back, looking at the countryside. It was bleak and the wind made a low moaning noise. I'd have felt scared if I hadn't been used to bad weather in cyclo-crosses.

"Well, I got back on my bike and I got to the top of the col. There's a tunnel at the top and I asked a soigneur how far down I was on the leader. He told me six minutes. I found van Hauwaert at the exit of the tunnel with his bike in his hand and a cloak on his back. He told me he was packing it in. I was beyond feeling happy about it and I just got on with going down through the snow that lay on the road on that side of the mountain.

"The view was totally different now. The snow made the countryside beautiful. The sky was really clear. But now it was my turn to have trouble. It was hard to keep going. In places there were 20 cm of snow and sometimes more. Each time I was obliged to get off and push. It was cyclo-cross—off, on, riding, walking. I could keep going but it was slowing me right down. Then I had to stop with stomach cramp. Doubled up, one hand on my bike and the other on my stomach, I collapsed on to a rock on the left side of the road. I was bitter with cold. All I could do was move my head a little from left to right and right to left.

"I saw a little house not far away but I couldn't get there. I didn't realise just what danger I was in. I just had one thought: to get to San Remo first and I attached no importance to the pain I felt … I thought too of my contract with the bike factory. I'd get double my wages if won as well as primes and there'd be my 300 francs for first place. Happily in my misfortune a man chanced to pass by.

"'*Signor, signor…*'

"He stopped and spoke to me in Italian, naturally. I nodded towards the house and said *casa* and he understood. He took me by the right arm while I leaned my left on my bike. The house was a tiny inn. The boss undressed me completely and wrapped me in a blanket. I murmured *aqua caldo* and pointed at the bottles of rum.

"I did some physical exercises and my life started to come back. I wanted to go on but the *patron* wouldn't hear of it and pointed at the snow still falling outside. And then first van Hauwaert and then Ernest Paul came in. They were so frozen that they put their hands into the flames. Ernest Paul had lost a shoe without noticing.

"I was there for about 25 minutes. I saw four riders go by, or at least four piles of mud. I decided to press on. Ernest Paul said 'You're crazy.' And the innkeeper didn't want to let me go. I had to trick him by saying I could meet someone who would get me to San Remo by train. I set off and caught Cocchi and Pavesi and I got to the control just behind Ganna, who was setting off as I stopped. I set off again after Baugé told me I could win and I passed Ganna at the edge of the town. And I caught Albini a few kilometers later.

"At the control at Savona everybody was astonished to see me alone. The crowd didn't recognise me. I didn't stop long and I took Trouselier's spare bike, because I knew he and Garrigou had abandoned before Ovada. I was sure of my victory and with only 100 km to go I felt a new strength. The idea of crossing the line alone brought back all my energy. I got to San Remo well behind the scheduled time. It was 6 PM when I stopped underneath the blowing banner that showed the end of my Calvary."

And so the race ended, with riders scattered back as far as the Turchino and taking shelter where they could. Christophe spent a month in the hospital to recover from frost bite to his hands and the damage of the cold to his body. It was two years before he got back his original health. Only three riders finished and the result is still uncertain because some reports say van Hauwaert came fourth and others that he was disqualified for hanging on to a car.

The footnote is that things may not have changed as much as you think. Panic spread through the 2001 race when mudslides and torrential rain closed the Turchino just as it almost did in Christophe's day. Maybe the organisers learned from the events of 1910. They could have sent their riders across the mountain. They didn't. Because men like Christophe aren't born any more.

11

HOW TO MAKE A COMMOTION

The Tour de France finished every year from 1903 to 1967 on the shallow concrete bankings of the Parc des Princes to the west of Paris. The track has long since been demolished and the site is now the stadium of the Paris St-Germain soccer team. No spectacle there, though, could astonish the crowd as much as a curious happening in 1956.

One by one the surviving riders came back on to the track to ride their lap of honour. One by one their exploits, however humble, were expounded by the announcer and time after time the crowd cheered and waved. The biggest applause, of course, was for the French. And the biggest applause of all was for a humble team rider called Roger Hassenforder. Not because he'd won, because he'd come only 50th, the only time in five Tours that he even finished the race. No, they applauded because he took his lap of honour ... backwards. Not backwards in the sense of riding the track the wrong way round but backwards meaning that he was sitting on the handlebars and looking back towards the saddle as he pedalled, like a circus clown.

Roger Hassenforder, largely forgotten these days, was one of the sport's great entertainers. He won hearts more through his pranks than his results, although he did win seven stages of the Tour and once wore the yellow jersey. Perhaps he was just happy to be alive: as a boy in the Colmar region of eastern France he dug a hole in a field and buried wartime shells, other ammunition and cans of petrol. He boasted to friends of his "Hassenforder atom bomb" and lit a trail of gunpowder to demonstrate that it worked. He was running for the shelter of a trench when it blew up. It took intensive care by specialists in Switzerland to treat the burns on his legs and back.

"Hassen" became a cyclist when he was 19, having given up soccer. He was so far behind in his first race that the judges had gone home by the time he crossed the line. In his second, friends found him exhausted in a ditch. He'd taken only two oranges to eat in a race that was 200 km long.

He began training properly when he joined the army in 1950, then took the yellow jersey in the first week of the 1953 Tour. In 1956 he won three stages. But what people remember are the jokes. For instance, justifiably expecting a tedious night at a UCI banquet in Paris, he rounded up a dozen pigeons and took them into the dining hall with him. When the droning and self-congratulation of the international officials became too much, he set them loose all at once. The birds panicked, flapped round the room above the heads of startled diners and then flew up to the roof and chandeliers. The chandeliers hadn't been dusted in years and the birds dislodged clouds of dust which for the next quarter of an hour fell on to the smart suits and dresses of the distinguished guests.

They weren't amused but antics like that made Hassenforder a great attraction to fans, who turned out to watch him ride criteriums. Again he didn't disappoint. His special trick was to grab women's hats as he passed, a trick that delighted time after time but one day went horribly wrong when he found out too late that the woman had tied her bonnet under her chin. She was yanked forward by her head, Hassenforder wobbling dangerously in the tight bunch … and the trick was never repeated.

These days Hassenforder relaxes in the restaurant and hotel called Chez Roger Hassenforder that he founded in a timbered 17th-century building in Kaysersberg, Colmar. The sign outside shows a rider in a yellow jersey riding an ancient bike with a huge front wheel and a tiny one trailing it. His home is full of skins and stuffed animals from his career as a big-game hunter. "Such things were permitted then," he says.

12

HOW TO LEAVE THINGS UNTIL THE LAST MOMENT

If the Dutch have a reputation, it's for quiet innovation, open-mindedness, a sense of organisation and an irritating desire to feel superior to everyone else. It all shows in the unrelenting neatness of their country and its design-it-by-numbers housing areas, the Nursery School style of lettering on the road signs and the proliferation of marijuana cafés in Amsterdam.

You'd expect Holland's one big road race to be distinctive as well, then. Distinctive but not too distinctive, in the Dutch way. It should all run perfectly, like their trains and their to-the-second timekeeping.

Well …

The Amstel Gold Race was the idea of two colourful entrepreneurs called Ton Vissers and Herman Krott, who ran a company called Inter Sport. Vissers was a former house decorator and hockey player from Rotterdam. In 1963 he managed a no-hope team in the Tour of Holland. He was as useless at his job as his riders were at theirs. Legend says that when he heard while following the break that one of his riders had punctured in the bunch, he turned in the road and drove back towards the race. Officials flung him out. He must have learned, though, because in 1966 he became manager of Willem II, Holland's only pro team worth the name until TI-Raleigh a decade later.

Krott ran a car-parts firm called HeKro and worked as Peter Post's personal assistant because he idolised the man. He came from Amsterdam and Post—one of the world's leading six-day riders—from the suburb of Amstelveen.

Inter Sport soon began running more than two dozen well-paying road races a year, plus more on the track, the best professional calendar that little Holland had had in decades. But their races weren't classics of the sort they had over the border in Belgium, like the Tour of Flanders and Liège–Bastogne–Liège. Finally Krott used his links with the Amstel beer company, for which he'd been a representative, and set up the Amstel pro team and then in 1966 announced the first Amstel Gold Race.

It would be the queen of races, he said, run on Koninginnedag—the Dutch queen's special day—on April 30. It would start in Amsterdam and cover 280 km before finishing close to the German border at Maastricht. Prizes were set at about $7,000 by today's prices. *Wielersport,* the shabby magazine that the Dutch federation used to list races, exceptionally dull items of official news and alarmingly long lists of suspensions, said it would be "of great international allure."

What seems not to have happened is the obvious step of looking at an atlas to see if the route was actually possible. Holland is very flat and has to be constantly drained. It is riddled with rivers, streams, ditches and canals and so a race from Amsterdam to Maastricht was a mite fanciful. It would be an endless zigzag from one bridge to the next, not just a long scribble of a route forever turning corners but considerably longer than 280 km, which was already a long way.

Krott and Vissers switched their plans to Utrecht, then to Rotterdam. Maastricht was dropped in favour of the unknown village of Meerssen. And finally all looked settled. But then 20 days before the race, the pair realised they hadn't got permission to cross the Moerdijk bridge. Since Moerdijk was the only way out of Rotterdam to the south, the omission was significant.

They never did get permission, either, so with 19 days to go the whole race had to be redrawn, police forces begged for help, road closures negotiated. The start shifted to Breda, a long way south and approaching the Belgian border and down in the area where northern Dutchmen think the locals little better than cross-eyed, straw-sucking yokels. By then the police weren't happy, there or anywhere else, because the Provos, militant hippies, had declared Holland a state of anarchy. What's more, the Dutch had changed their mind about the royal family that the race was supposed to be celebrating and they were taking to the street because the queen's daughter, Beatrix, planned to marry a German, Claus von Amsberg. The German occupation and the cruelty and starvation it produced hadn't slipped the public memory.

The race was set for April 30. On April 26, Vissers and Krott called it off. Riders were told to stay at home, a press conference was called, the news was broken to the rest of the world and attempts were made to placate disappointed fans. Or ... they were about to be. The organisers had only just started explaining the situation when the Dutch roads ministry in The Hague called to say the race could go ahead after all—provided the organisers promised never again to run it on Koninginnedag.

The classic that almost never was finally took place. There were no serious protests and people were so pleased with it, even though it was won by a Frenchman (Jean Stablinski), that they forgot about the roads minister and the promise they'd made. The race never did start in Amsterdam, Rotterdam or Utrecht and it never again started in Breda. It did finally get to finish in Maastricht from 1992, though, and since 1998 it's also started there.

It avoids criss-crossing hundreds of canal and river bridges by staying in the single hilly area in the south-east. But one problem has simply been replaced by another. A crowded country has a lot of traffic and little car-parking space. The roads are closed for the race but people living along the course are allowed to park their cars on the road. On top of that, the route is full of traffic-calming humps, chicanes and small roundabouts. They make it as dangerous as the cobbled hills of the Tour of Flanders but in some ways worse because many of the obstacles come unpredictably on the riders.

Inter Sport, which started the race, wound up in 1970 and Herman Krott ran the race alone until 1995. It's now run by Leo van Vliet, one of the riders in the Raleigh team run by Peter Post—the very man whom Herman Krott worshipped all that time earlier and the team that succeeded Ton Vissers' Willem II. It may be risky, but no more ramshackle than its origins.

13

HOW NOT TO BE AN OFFICIAL (1)

The Amstel Gold Race is slick and so now are world championships. They are polished promotions. But they haven't always been that way, especially at first. Take Cologne in 1895, for instance. The big event as usual was the sprint, in which Robert Protin of Belgium was riding against George Banker, the son of an American tycoon, and another Belgian, called Huet. Protin, a man with a little moustache, lined up closest to the starter. Everyone was tense because in those days sprinting was the cream of the sport and this was the final, the crème de la crème.

One of the most tense was the starter. Overcome by nerves, he waved down the starting flag and poked it into Protin's eye. The Belgian, predictably, didn't win. The winner was the American, Banker, and he cared so little about what had happened to Protin that he set off on his victory lap while the unhappy Belgian was rubbing away the pain. The crowd, though, wasn't so happy, and neither were the Belgian officials nor, presumably, the starter. The judges, managers and anyone else who cared to join in immediately went into a huddle and eventually they told the riders they had to compete again.

Banker said he wouldn't.

"You will," retorted the judges.

"I won't," said Banker.

"Then you won't be world champion," the judges threatened, and so the American got back on his bike, lined up once more against Huet and Protin and the race was flagged away without incident. Protin, despite a bloodshot and swollen eye, won and became world champion. And did Banker settle for that? No, he didn't. Anything but a good loser and, because he had no more convincing reason, he complained that he'd been demoralised. The crowd and then the officials, who until then had been behind Protin, began to swing behind Banker. The International Cycling Association, which ran the sport in those days, debated the issue for weeks. Finally it said both races would be cancelled and there'd be another. The riders didn't have time to react before the whole Belgian nation, represented by its cycling federation, said it would leave the ICA if its man's claim to the title wasn't recognised.

The ICA couldn't risk that because it didn't have the status and authority that the UCI has these days and Belgium could easily have started a breakaway faction. The ICA shrugged and said Protin could stay world champion and that was the end of it. Protin became Belgian national champion in 1891, 1892, 1893 and 1894, won the national 100 km title in 1893, the European sprint championship in 1892 and 1893, the French open 5 km championship in 1893, and took the world 500 m record in 1895. You can't help thinking he deserved to win the world title. He died in Liège in 1953 when he was 82.

But if his case is comical, what of Willie Falk Hansen and Lucien Michard? Their world sprint championship was in Denmark in 1931. Hansen was the local man and Michard a Frenchman who'd won the previous four years. There were just two men in their final and the starter managed to set them off without mishap. The judge, Albert Colignon, watched them circle the track until they reached the last 200 meters. He remembered who was on the inside and who on the outside and he fixed his eyes on the line ready to do what judges do, which was to judge. Luckily for him, the result was clear and he announced Hansen as world champion.

But he wasn't. Even the Danish crowd, which would have loved Hansen to have won, could see he'd been beaten. Shouts of protest went up, arms were waved and things thrown on to the track. Colignon was baffled and distraught. He looked first one way and then the other for an explanation. And then dawned the horrible truth: the two had changed sides in the last 200 meters, the rider on the left now being on the right as they crossed the line. It was Michard's wheels he'd seen come first and not Hansen.

Colignon felt stupid but it was an understandable if massive mistake and he was happy to own up. The trouble was that the UCI in those days insisted that a judge's result couldn't be changed, even if everyone knew it was wrong. Hansen had been named world champion and the rules said nothing could be done about it. He got the champion's jersey he didn't deserve and he wore it for the rest of the year.

And Michard? Well, he was happy for Hansen. He soon realised the opportunity it offered him, how he could make more money from being cheated of a championship than he would have done from winning it. He made himself a champion's jersey of his own design and he and Hansen went on a season of grudge matches all over Europe and raked in the cash in revenge matches.

14

HOW NOT TO BE AN OFFICIAL (2)

There is a belief in Britain that time-trials are a race of truth. It's a view shared by some riders as well, but for the British there's a lot of self-justification because for almost a century Britain allowed nothing but solo racing against the clock. Conventional races were banned because back at the end of the 19th century a group of racers north of London had upset a posh woman on a horse. She had complained to the police, who already took a dim view of bike racing, and cycling officials panicked and banned all racing on the roads for fear that it would lead to a ban on all cyclists.

Little by little rebels began organising time-trials at country crossroads soon after dawn. The details were kept secret even in cycling magazines, lists of riders were headed "Private and Confidential", competitors were ordered to dress in black from neck to toe to make them "inconspicuous" and nobody carried a number. They were compelled to carry bells to show how responsible they were, and officials stood at road junctions to be sure that riders obeyed the "stop" signs at 5 AM. Events were called not races but, to disguise their purpose, time "trials"—tests of something or other but certainly not races, constable.

Emergency measures have a habit of not going away, though, and before long the British began not only to like time-trialling but to see it as superior to the flashy, trivial Continental style of racing in which, they believed, all you had to do was sit in a big group of riders and then sprint past them at the end. The British, they insisted, were the only true racers and they developed codes of behaviour around their races and a very strict view of the way riders were to compete alone and be well separated on the road, of how nobody could follow by car, and above all of how money was never to change hands in prizes, only bits of bikes or perhaps a canteen of cutlery or a clock. The rules on amateurism were so strict that a rider could be declared professional if the maker's name on his bicycle was visible in photographs.

Given all this moral superiority, the British were naturally delighted when Denmark decided to run the world championship as a time-trial in 1931. Such a thing hadn't happened since 1921, when Britain ran the championships and British riders took the first three places. (By contrast, the track championships were so badly organised that the UCI took them away halfway through and finished them in Paris, the track near Liverpool being so slippery in the rain and so bumpy in the dry that it was considered dangerous.) Denmark, clearly, had seen the light of reason and logic which the British believed unique to themselves and Britain decided to send its star men, Freddy Frost, Len Cave and Frank Southall, with F.T. Brown (initials were common) as reserve.

The magazine *Cycling*, which had become the greatest missionary for time-trialling and against the heathen Continental racing, triumphed: "The world's amateur road race championship is absurdly simple this year … It is, therefore, perfectly easy to jot down the English times, note the best times abroad over the distance, and announce the result long before the starter has given the Danish equivalent for the word 'go'!"

There was some irony but the headline still read:

IF PERFECTLY FIT
Southall Will Win The World's
Road Championship,
predicts "The Loiterer"

The Loiterer was disappointed. The race was a disaster. The police didn't close the roads and anybody could follow the race. Faster riders caught up the slower ones and got tangled up in the convoys of following cars and other riders. Even purists like Frank Southall, who'd have been horrified by this breach of purity, accepted he had sat on a wheel for 30 km.

"The whole race was as badly organised as a road time-trial could be and was a disgrace," *Cycling* sniffed.

Things were no better at the finish. Excited crowds milled around the timekeeper so that he couldn't see the riders as they crossed the line. Their numbers were shouted in one language and then translated into others before they reached him. He didn't see Southall at all but the British timed him at 5:6:26. The timekeeper left off the seconds and wrote down 5:6. At least five others got the wrong times and it was anybody's guess who'd done what.

Cycling's man on the spot reported: "A time was recorded against a competitor's number given as 53. About that moment I had myself observed a rider crossing the line carrying the number 66 (Olmo, Italy). Three-quarters of an hour later an Italian delegate approached the timekeeper's table and for some moments completely monopolised the attention of the officials whilst he claimed that Olmo had arrived and that he had crossed the line 'one second after Henry Hansen.' After some minutes of heated discussion in French, Italian, Danish (and I could not resist saying a word, too), the time previously recorded against 53 was transferred to 66 and Olmo was listed second in the Amateur Road Championship of the world."

The next sentence is almost plaintive.

"What happened to No. 53, T. Wanzenried, of Switzerland, I cannot say. He is not shown on the finishing list at all."

One good thing did come out of it, though. Among those watching the professional race, which was much better run because the officials had learned from the debâcle of the amateurs, were the French journalists Gaston Bénac and Albert Baker d'Isy. They had never seen a top-class professional time-trial before because in those days there was no world championship and also no time-trials in the Tour de France.

The two men worked for the newspaper *Paris-Soir*, Bénac as its beret-wearing sports editor and Baker d'Isy as his star writer. They watched in admiration as Learco Guerra of Italy won the title after riding 170 km at 35.2 km/h. And there and then they decided that what they wanted, and what their paper could organise, was an annual international time-trial that they could bill as a revenge match for the world championship, which of course would normally be run *en ligne*.

Baker d'Isy suggested the name "Grand Prix des Nations" and it became just what the two hoped, not just a revenge match but th virtual world time-trial championship. Among those it introduced to a startled public was the youthful Jacques Anquetil, who won in 1953 when he was a barely known 19-year-old from the Rouen countryside and only a semi-professional. Anquetil won every year from 1953 to 1958, then again in 1961, 1965 and 1966. He was never beaten and his record is never likely to be bettered.

Anquetil is dead now, and so is the Grand Prix des Nations. But the world has a time-trial championship and, while nobody would have dreamed of it at the time, it was all thanks to the Danes. Oh, and the British, by the way, still cling to their love of solo races at dawn. Although they no longer have to carry bells.

15

HOW TO WIN A CLASSIC

It's never too far to go to see a good bike race. You don't often come home disappointed. But equally you don't often come home with as much to talk about as the fans who paid to sit in the vélodrome to wait for the finish of Paris–Roubaix in 1949.

There's more to a day at Roubaix than just the finish of the mud-and-blood stars who've ridden from the capital. There is a program of minor races and constant news of the stars of the road who all that time are getting closer and closer. These days the crowd can see the same television pictures that you and I see at home, but in 1949 there was no live television coverage and so all afternoon the crowd strained to hear the telephoned bulletins read out over the loudspeakers. The fans knew what was happening on the road, that the leaders were entering the city, that they were approaching the track, that they were about to burst through the square tunnel that led to their last laps around the track. And they were on the edges of their seats with excitement.

Would it be one man alone, or a group? Would they be all outsiders or would the stars be there? Would their favourite be there? The tension was unbearable. Imagine that crowd in 1949, therefore, staring at the way into the track only to be distracted by a growing commotion from people who were looking elsewhere. Nervously, because they didn't want to miss anything, they turned their eyes from the track entrance and looked for what was causing the fuss. And then, to their disbelief, they saw the race leaders coming on to the track by a side entrance, looking around to see where the finish line might be, then racing off again.

No race has ever finished in greater chaos. To this day the Paris–Roubaix of 1949 has two winners. The winners finished separately, they were separated by four other riders and they both reached the line by different routes. It took two international conferences to sort what to do about it.

What the crowd knew was that three riders had reached the entrance to the track together. There had been no time to report, though, that an official had gestured them down a side-road intended only for officials' cars and that the riders had gone that way instead. André Mahé, Jacques Moujica and Frans Leenen soon realised something had gone wrong and they looked for somewhere to go. But the road was narrow, it was filling with other traffic, and sorting out the error wasn't simple.

Moujica turned a tight circle, lost his balance, fell off and broke a pedal. Mahé and Leenen rode beneath the cliff-like concrete face of the outside of the track, looking for a way in, and in frustration opted for a small gate which, well, just happened to be there. And that was how they reached the banking, pushing through whatever and whomever they had to push through, then sprinting for the line.

"*C'est trop bête d'en parler* [it's just too stupid to talk about]," Mahé said as we sat around a low table beside the kitchen, where his wife was making us pancakes and coffee. "There was a break. [Serse] Coppi attacked. His brother Fausto gave him a push to get him away. He wanted his brother to win. I waited a bit and then I attacked and I caught him and the break. Then I went off by myself. I was going to win Paris–Roubaix. At the entrance to the vélodrome, there were crowds everywhere, blocking the way. I looked around for where to go and I was directed round the outside wall of the track, to where the team cars had to park. It wasn't like nowadays, when there's television and everything. Then it was more chaotic and the whole road was blocked.

"People said I should have known the way into the track. But how do you know a thing like that at the end of Paris–Roubaix, when you've raced all day over roads like that? A gendarme signaled the way to go and that's the way I went. Of course, the police never apologized afterwards.

"It was a journalist on a motorbike who managed to get up to me. He was shouting 'Not that way! Not that way!' And I turned round in the road and I rode back beneath the outside wall of the grandstand and I saw a gateway that went into the track, a gateway for journalists. And that's the way I went, except that it came out on the other side of the track from the proper entrance. The bunch came in and Serse won the sprint. But then his brother told Serse to go to the judges to object. He told Serse that I hadn't ridden the entire and precise course and that therefore I should be *déclassé*. But that was below him.

"Coppi wanted his brother to have a big victory. He was a great champion, Coppi, but to do what he did, to protest like that to get a victory for his brother, that wasn't dignified for a champion. That was beneath him. A champion like that should never have stooped that low. I never spoke to him about it. Never did. Why should I?

"It marked me, though, and I still feel marked by it. I was alone. I would have won alone. I had attacked alone and Serse couldn't follow me. I had received my bouquet and I was even in the shower when I heard the news. For me, I had won Paris–Roubaix."

The judge, Henri Boudard, sent him on his lap of honour. What else could he do? But Serse wasn't going to be persuaded he hadn't won. He knew there were other riders ahead of him but he protested that he was the winner, that the others hadn't completed the course and that he had. Novel though using another gate might be, it wasn't part of the official route. He was sorry for them but they should be disqualified or demoted. No question about it.

Boudard wavered and then sided with Coppi. It was perfectly true that Mahé and the others hadn't followed the right course, and that's the least a judge should ask of competitors. So he named Coppi the winner.

"I only followed the rules," Boudard protested as the world surrounded him with angry gestures (Frenchmen, Belgians) and grateful smiles (Italians). The organisers couldn't miss the commotion and compromised. The judges could decide what they wanted but they would give Mahé and the others the prizes they would have won. Five days later the French federation followed suit and confirmed Mahé as winner. "It couldn't be otherwise," said Achille Joinard, the French cycling president.

"It certainly can!" the Italians protested and they appealed to the

UCI. Now, the race was in April. It took from then until August for the UCI to decide it had no option but to cancel the race and make neither man the winner. A non-race, a rejection of responsibility, wasn't an answer, though. It was a decision to please nobody. The UCI, now as unhappy as Mahé, Coppi and the French and Italian federations, said it would make a proper and final decision in November. The French then poured insults on Joinard's head. They called him a traitor for going back on the decision to award the race to a Frenchman and accused him of soft-pedalling Mahé's cause because he didn't want to spoil his chances of becoming UCI president. That gave the scandal fresh spin. It also made a decision impossible and in November the UCI said both riders had won. And that's the way it remains until this day, officialdom unable to decide whether coming into the track one way rather than another was as good as following the official route.

"Thank heavens there's another Paris–Roubaix in four months," said one official.

16

HOW TO GET THROUGH THE MOUNTAINS (1)

In the old days there were prizes for riders who could get through the mountains of the Tour de France without getting off their bikes. Gustave Garrigou, for example, remembered winning five sovereigns for being alone in not walking on the Tourmalet.

Well, it's easy to think that just because bikes and roads have improved since then that it's become easier to ride the Alps and Pyrenees. But it ain't necessarily so, as the old song put it. Sometimes riders need a return to the tradition of spectators pushing the lesser-lights as they pass. And sometimes spectators themselves need to be encouraged to break what is now a well-applied rule that they should keep their hands to themselves.

Which brings us to Bernard Sainz. These days he is better known as Dr. Mabuse, the man behind the revival of many riders' careers by techniques he insists are no more than homeopathy. In 1976 he was a soigneur for the GAN-Mercier team, sponsored by an insurance company and a bike builder and led by Raymond Poulidor with the Dutchman Joop Zoetemelk. Unnoticed in that year's Tour team of 10 was the Frenchman Michel Perin, number 26. He would never be a winner but he was an excellent team-rider and a man on whom Poulidor and Zoetemelk depended and that was why he was included. That willingness to sacrifice his own chances for his leaders meant he wasn't, therefore, a lesser-light to be abandoned after he crashed going down the first mountain in the Alps.

It was Sainz's job to patch his wounds and put him back on his bike, but Perin had a lot of pain, there were three more cols to come, and he was in for a long, lonely and painful ride. Now, in the GAN team car with Sainz was one of the race commissaires, officials who often hitched rides with managers and soigneurs to see what they got up to and that they stayed within the rules. That limited the ruses Sainz could get up to. But it didn't stop some quick thinking.

"In my youth," he recalled, "I took part in a number of car rallies and I have to say that I was as happy on four wheels as I had been on two [Sainz was a talented amateur track rider until a bad crash], perhaps even more daring. Going down the col, I dropped back from the other vehicles, feigning lack of attention, making a show of retuning my car radio, and I lit a cigarillo. Then, suddenly, I accelerated to catch the other cars. I let the ash from the cigarillo drop on to my trousers during the straight stretches, and I'd look down to brush it away and straighten up only as we went into the next bend."

He skidded round bends all the way down the mountain, driving like a demon, squealing the tires until the commissaire begged to be let out. "I'd been warned that you drove too fast but this is more than I can bear," he sobbed. Sainz apologised profusely, hoped he hadn't upset the man's day and grinned to himself as he pushed the door open for him to step out.

Now Sainz could start looking after the cut, bruised and suffering Perin in the way that he wanted to. Which wasn't necessarily the orthodox way. First he stopped at a bar and asked for several waiters' notepads. Then he drove two hairpins ahead of Perin, on that col and on the others that day. He smiled as his rider regained the *grupetto*, the bunch of non-climbers who ride just fast enough to finish within the time limit. He had kept him in the race. That night he could do some proper work on the cuts and scrapes.

That evening Perin came to see Sainz.

"It was unbelievable," he said. "I hardly had to pedal when I was riding those cols behind you. All the spectators were pushing me."

"You're joking," Sainz insisted with a straight face.

"No, no, honestly, it's true."

Sainz kept his poker expression. "No, it can't be. They only push the last rider. You just recovered without being aware of it. It's a tribute to your willpower."

Perin must have found out the truth some time so I can tell you it now: Sainz had used his notepads to write over and over: "The rider behind me has a fever-pitch temperature. Please give him a push." Then he'd handed them out to every group of fans he'd passed. Perin, as he said himself, had hardly had to pedal. And, as he said, he had recovered without being aware of it—although because of wiliness and quick thinking rather than willpower.

17

HOW TO GET THROUGH THE MOUNTAINS (2)

But how did the mountains get in the Tour de France in the first place? Henri Desgrange didn't really want them, after all. He sent his riders over the Ballon d'Alsace in 1906 in the expectation that few of them would be able to ride over it. Maybe none of them, which is what he boasted would happen. In fact René Pottier, a dour and suicidal man, rode all the way without stopping. It gave him tendinitis, but he did it. Desgrange thought that was bad enough; the idea of the Alps and the Pyrenees with their mighty altitudes and barely-mapped goat tracks just terrified him.

Nevertheless, the fact that Pottier rode all the way up the Ballon hides a more obvious point—that others didn't. Desgrange loved the struggle of man to become superman and Pottier satisfied him. But equally, if even Pottier had walked up the Ballon, Desgrange wouldn't have had a bike race. It'd have become a walking race, so still hillier territory was out of the question. Even Desgrange's lust for excess didn't extend to riders dying of exposure and exhaustion or a bike race where people walked most of the way.

The man who changed his mind after a lot of angry arguments was called Adolphe Steinès. He worked with Desgrange in the offices of *L'Auto* in the rue faubourg Montmartre in Paris's 9th *arrondissement* and by late middle age he'd become a jovial-looking, round-faced man with circular spectacles and an air of good living. Desgrange by contrast had a long bony face with high cheek bones and sunken cheeks.

Steinès argued all through 1909 that Desgrange should expand his horizons. Often it made both men angry. We know how angry because Steinès himself remembered the conversation:

"*Patron*, I'll give you a plan to make the Tour still bigger this year," he said late in the year.

"Bigger? You think it's not big enough already?"

"No. We've got to touch all the frontiers."

"Frontiers … frontiers … Your idea of going to Metz four years ago wasn't exactly brilliant."

"How do you mean? Not brilliant?"

"The German government ended up by banning it … No, Steinès, the mistake is in not staying strictly in France."

"Ah, there *patron*, I don't agree. You know very well that all our neighbours want us to visit them."

"I know. But it's not always easy. How about Spain?"

Desgrange was thinking of the Pyrenees. It's impossible to get from France to Spain without crossing them.

"Exactly," Steinès beamed. "Spain! I think we'd be able to cross the Pyrenees."

"The Pyrenees? You're joking." Desgrange turned his back in despair at his madman of an assistant. But Steinès wasn't joking and he argued so long that in the end Desgrange gave in. But not before he'd told Steinès: "You want me to kill them!"

Steinès smirked at his success, then went to his office and got out a map of southern France and the route of the Tour. And then, drawing a wavy line on the chart, he diverted the stage from Nîmes to Toulouse to Perpignan. Going there through Luchon and Bayonne would take the race over the cols de Peyresourde, Aspin, Tourmalet and Aubisque. Hardly a tentative first trial at real mountain riding.

Having done that, he took the map back to his boss, spread the map on the table and awaited the eruption he knew would come. It came.

"How can you dare to say it'd be a success?", Desgrange exploded. "You're going through places that don't exist."

"What doesn't exist?"

"What I say … that they don't exist. To climb as far as your cols [the col is the summit of a pass, although the word is often used now to mean the whole ascent], there isn't even a road."

"No road? What do you know about it?"

Steinès insisted he knew the area. Desgrange grew still angrier and, in a fury, told Steinès that if he was so convinced, he could go and look for himself. He was glad to be rid of the man and his crazy ideas.

So Steinès went to Pau in the south-west. Forty kilometers from there on the Gave de Pau river is the religious centre of Lourdes where the Virgin Mary led the peasant Bernadette Soubirous to the healing springs of the Grotte de Massabielle in 1858. If you cross the river in Pau and go the same distance south, you reach a junction at Laruns, from where what is now the D918 wiggles east through Eaux-Bonnes and over the col d'Aubisque.

Steinès called on a man called Blanchet, the local engineer of bridges and roads. The official listened amazed to his story and then told him the staff of *L'Auto* must all have gone mad to consider the Aubisque. The staff of *L'Auto*, of course, hadn't considered the Aubisque at all. Only Steinès had considered it.

"Do you *know* the Aubisque?" Blanchet asked.

"Of course," said Steinès airily. "I've just been up there. It's obvious that in the state it's in now, the Tour couldn't go up there. But you're going to arrange it."

"Me? But I haven't got a sou for that."

"No money? Ah well, too bad, I'll get you what you think necessary. How much do you think it would cost?"

Blanchet guessed 5,000 francs. It was more than Steinès had imagined and he said he'd have to phone Desgrange in Paris. He motioned to Blanchet to pick up the extension and together they heard Desgrange thunder: "Five thousand francs? But you're mad! You want to ruin us? I'll give you 1,500, not a centime more."

"Excellent," said Steinès, shouting to pretend that he had a bad line. "Did you say 2,000?" And he put the phone down. That night Steinès and Blanchet had dinner, Blanchet insisted the job couldn't be done for less than 5,000 and Steinès winked and said he'd find the rest "in an old drawer somewhere."

That sorted out the Aubisque—the Tour de France was going to pay for the road—but the Tourmalet was different. It's higher and snow-covered for much of the year. No snow-sweepers in those days, remember, for the simple reason that there was no road over the Tourmalet to sweep. It was no more than a goat track used by the only people who needed goat tracks: goat herds.

Steinès knew he could do no more until the worst of the snow had gone and he returned to Paris. He came back a month before the Tour. This time he went to the other side of Lourdes and into Sainte-Marie-de-Campan, the little village at the foot of the Tourmalet where years later Eugène Christophe would have to mend his forks on the village forge. There he had sausage, ham and cheese at an inn opposite the church and with the help of the landlady arranged to hire a driver called Dupont from Bagnères-de-Bigorre, the town he'd passed through to reach Ste-Marie-de-Campan.

The Tourmalet is 19 km long, rising around 1,200 m straight from the village. It runs in a series of hard and then easier slopes before a beak of a twist that starts the real climb at what is now the ski resort of La Mongie. It was there that Dupont's car grumbled to a halt in the snow. Steinès persuaded the driver to walk with him but after 600 meters he said he had had enough and he turned back.

"It's not a joke, the snow," he shouted. "The bears come over from Spain when it snows. It's six o'clock. It'll be dark soon. I'm not going any further." If Steinès was stupid enough to press on, he could do it alone. Dupont told him to look out for four-meter poles that showed the middle of the road in the snow and started to walk back to his car.

"Wait for me in Barèges," Steinès called back, referring to the far side of the mountain. Dupont said he would but warned Steinès that he was in for a dangerous 12 km walk, going up beyond 2,000 meters. He looked once more at Steinès in his city clothes, overcoat and ordinary leather shoes, dismissed him once more as a madman, and reversed his car with a lot of wheel-spinning and disappeared. Steinès grasped his walking stick and set off into the snow.

It didn't take long to feel less confident. And to grow scared. To his surprise, he heard voices above the low moaning of the icy wind. Now his heart was as frozen as his hands and ears. Who would wait on a mountain for travellers by night, and why? Were bandits he could hear likely to be worse than bears that he couldn't hear? He braced himself for an attack he felt sure would come and then felt a surge of relief when he found no more than youngsters watching sheep with their dog.

Steinès called to one. "Son, do you know the Tourmalet well?"

"Certainly," the boy said.

"Could you guide me?"

"Well..."

"I'll give you 20 francs and a gold coin. When we get to the other top, I'll give you another one."

"I don't need money," the boy said.

"But everyone needs money," Steinès said with astonishment, more used to hard-nosed Parisians than innocent mountain peasants.

"Well, I don't," the boy said. "But I'll take you anyway."

They took two and a half hours to walk the two kilometers to the col. By then night had fallen, dark, cloudy and with neither moon nor stars. Steinès wanted the boy to go further but he insisted on going back to his sheep, saying he'd get a beating if he didn't. He turned back downhill into the darkness and Steinès rested on a rock, now tired and terrified at what he'd done. He considered sitting it out until dawn, then realised he'd freeze to death before he saw it.

He walked on once more, downhill now but still slipping on the icy track. Even with his stick to steady him, he fell and began tumbling like a snowball. He came to a rest in a mountain stream, soaked now as well as cold. He climbed back to the road and again fell into the snow, exhausted. He found a *borne*, a milestone, and just sat and cried with relief, not because he was saved but simply because he'd once more found the track, which he thought he'd never see again. Then he pressed on, blind in the shadow of the mountain.

Hours later, exhausted and stumbling, he heard an adult voice.

"Who's that?" it demanded.

Steinès said nothing.

"Tell me who goes there or I'll shoot."

"I'm a lost traveller. I've just come across the Tourmalet."

The other voice changed to relief.

"Oh, it's you, Monsieur Steinès! We were expecting you!"

"Expected? How do you mean?"

"We got a phone call at Ste-Marie-de-Campan. Everybody's at Barèges. It's coming on for three o'clock. There are search teams of guides out looking for you." Barèges had its lights on as villagers waited for the madman they knew was crossing the mountain by foot. Steinès shuffled into the village and was greeted by the local writer for *L'Auto*, a man called Lanne-Camy.

"My dear Steinès, what a state you're in!" he said with some understatement. He took him for a bath and new clothes, too large but welcome.

"I promised to telegram Desgrange," Steinès told Lanne-Camy once he'd recovered.

"And what are you going to tell him?" the correspondent wanted to know, well aware that Desgrange wasn't going to be the easiest man to tell about such dangerous folly.

"I don't know yet. I've got to think about it. Have you got some paper?"

Lanne-Camy found some.

Steinès sucked on the end of his pencil, looked thoughtfully at his host and then said: "Tell me, old chap. Is the road good at the top when the snow has melted?"

"The road? But it's just a mule track!"

Steinès hesitated without speaking.

"What are you going to wire?" Lanne-Camy asked.

"*Je ne sais pas*", Steinès answered. "*Ah! Tant pis! A la grâce de Dieu…*" ("I don't know. Oh, hell … may God save me…")

And he applied the pencil to the paper.

"Henri Desgrange, *L'Auto*, Paris," he wrote. "Have crossed Tourmalet, stop. Very good road, stop. Perfectly feasible."

18

HOW TO (ALMOST) BAFFLE A SPANIARD

If you don't want to ride over mountains, or even in the rain, the thing to be is a track rider. You never have to clean your bike, you never have to go out in the rain and cold and you only ever have to turn left. The longest race you'd have to ride is a six-day, and there are ways of making that shorter than it's supposed to be as well.

One of the last six-days to drop the formula of six days' non-stop riding was Madrid. Everywhere else settled for a break during the night and, eventually, for no racing in the mornings either. There were no crowds then so why put on a show for no audience? But Madrid was more traditional and insisted riders stay on the track through the small hours, even if the racing was neutralised and competitors shuffled round reading newspapers, chatting or shaving. Some even turned their handlebars up the other way or steered with one foot. It wasn't as exhausting as racing but it was still wearing if you'd rather be in bed.

But, as I said, there are ways to get round it if you're crafty …

Tom Simpson was contracted to ride Madrid with an Australian rider, John Tressider. He took with him an amateur enthusiast called David Nice, who'd met Simpson while racing in Belgium. The two had got on well and Nice went to Madrid to see six-day racing from the inside and to earn himself some money with Simpson and Tressider.

After a night or two of boring riding round the track at night, Simpson spotted the obvious: that Nice had the same lean face and rudder-like nose. In fact, that if he dressed up as Simpson, he could very well pass for him in a dull light. And so, the idea born, he put him in his own tracksuit, wrapped a scarf round the bottom of his face (which riders did anyway because there was no heating in the stadium at night) and topped him off with a Russian hat he had bought years earlier at a big race in Moscow.

"He was me to anyone giving a cursory glance at the figures plodding round the track," he recalled.

Nice was nervous but either nobody spotted the trick or they were prepared to stay quiet about it. More confident now, he rode round and round the track as Simpson got a night's sleep. The other riders must have known what was going on and they may even have objected to rivals being in bed while they had to ride, but they'd also have enjoyed the mischief and the way it cocked a snook at the organisers and their outdated rules.

Unfortunately, the track manager was also a cyclist. He was in awe of the riders, to whom he couldn't talk in the height of the battle, and he was prepared to stay up at night to meet them. Simpson was a favourite because he was a character and talkative, so what more natural that he should ride his own bike up to him and begin talking in the one language they shared?

Simpson remembered: "He chatted away quite happily to Dave, whose French was near enough non-existent. Well, it was not long before he sensed something was wrong and whipped the scarf off the poor lad's face. He stormed over to my cabin and dragged me out, half asleep, on to the track. That was that! He and the other officials kept their eyes on us after that and we had little chance of getting away with any more larks like that."

19

HOW TO BE A MISCHIEF

The Dutchman Rini Wagtmans fancied a prank, too, in 1969. Wagtmans, whose streak of white hair in the centre of his forehead gave him the nickname *Kuifje*, or Tufty, lives in the same village as Wim van Est, where he is the driving force behind the club there.

In 1969 he was about to finish sixth in the Tour de France, which was in its last two days. There was just a stage that led from Clermont-Ferrand, the Michelin tire-making town in eastern France, to Montargis and then a conventional race from Montargis to Créteil in the morning followed by the traditional time-trial into Paris in the afternoon. Wagtmans wasn't likely to win any of those or to improve on his overall position, so he had nothing to lose from a practical joke.

He chose the day's very first minutes, when the race was still ambling through Clermont-Ferrand before the *départ réel* in the outskirts. Riders were still discussing what they'd read in the papers and generally getting comfortable when they were startled to see a flash of royal blue. Wagtmans had broken away in his Willem II jersey.

Jacques Goddet watched astonished as the Dutchman raced up past his bright red car at the head of the race and he waved and sounded the horn to stop him pushing on towards the motorcycle outriders who were clearing a way through the city. But Wagtmans took no notice; he pushed his bike into the highest gear he could turn and raced through the streets like a demon. And then he spotted what he wanted: a side-turning. Out of sight of the others, he skidded to a halt, slipped his feet out of the toe clips and ran into the alleyway. And there he hid.

Back in the bunch, nobody knew what to do. Then the Frenchman Lucien Aimar, never a man to take offence lightly, set off in angry chase. Aimar was too good to be ignored and when he went, everyone else went as well. Riders at the front knew what was going on even if they didn't understand why. At the back, they had no idea. Those at the front were angry; those at the back found themselves clinging to a long snaking line of riders racing through a part of town they were supposed to negotiate gently. The speed grew faster and faster.

Wagtmans knew the fuss he would cause. What he hadn't forecast was that it would be so spectacular. What he'd planned was to wait until the field had trundled slowly past and then to tag on the back of the peloton and have a laugh with his pals. Instead, the race went so fast that he couldn't get back on his bike fast enough. Far from chuckling, he was reduced to chasing the race for kilometer after kilometer, his face grimacing and his teeth all but chewing the handlebar tape. Some stuffy souls thought that justice had been done.

20

HOW TO FALL OFF A RAINBOW

The saddest world champion in history is the Dutchman Harm Ottenbros. His world and life fell apart the moment that he pulled on his rainbow jersey at Zolder, in Belgium, on August 10, 1969. He thought he had moved from being an unknown 26-year-old criterium rider to one of the best recognised riders in the world, collecting a fortune wherever he rode. Instead, he became the world's most ridiculed "star" and within a few years he was living in a squat, sleeping on a floor and wishing he'd never been a cyclist.

The background to this curious tale lies in the opposing strengths of neighbouring nations. Holland had just one star worthy of winning the championship, Jan Janssen, but he was ill and he couldn't ride. Without him, the Dutch team was full of riders who'd normally expect little better in life than fetching bottles and giving their bosses a push or a tow when called on. On the other hand, Belgium had Eddy Merckx, and Eddy Merckx was so strong, so dominant in 1969 that other riders had grown bitter and determined that he shouldn't win and dominate cycling still further. The result was that every move he made was negated and he dismounted in despair to the whistles and jeering of fans who didn't understand what was happening.

Getting rid of Merckx had become more important than winning the race to many riders and they seemed confused or even relieved when Ottenbros rode away in the last four kilometers with a Belgian, Julien Stevens. It was as if they didn't know what to do; a star had been extinguished and now two unknowns had risen in his place. They stayed away until the line. Ottenbros won by centimeters and took what Jacques Anquetil, Gino Bartali, Sean Kelly and others never had: a world road title.

The world of cycling wasn't impressed. It turned on him. No matter that he had won as legitimately as anyone else, that the stars had been more occupied with their personal revenge than their own success. No, Ottenbros wasn't worthy of the rainbow jersey and the ridicule spread out from the professional bunch to organisers and fans. Ottenbros, whose life should have been made, earned no more as world champion than he had as a criterium rider. The only rider to congratulate him was Franco Bitossi and Ottenbros was so touched by his thought that he gave him one of his rainbow jerseys. The rest ganged up against him just as they had against Merckx, stopping him winning even criteriums. They jeered at his weakness on hills and called him The Eagle of Hogerheide, an ironic reference to the climber Federico Bahamontes, the Eagle of Toledo, and the unrelenting flatness of the Dutch countryside where Ottenbros lived.

"That nickname made me more famous than my world championship ever did," Ottenbros says now.

He couldn't defend his title because he broke his wrist in the Tour of Flanders at the start of the season. Then his team, Willem II, folded. Nobody else wanted him. Ottenbros retired, depressed, and considered suicide. In 1976 he rode to the Zeeland bridge in southwest Holland with Gerrie Knetemann, a rider of the new generation. He stopped, lifted his bike over the parapet and threw it down into the river. He watched it circle down through the water until it disappeared in the murky depths, then finished his journey sitting on the top tube of Knetemann's bike.

Things got worse. His marriage broke up and he lost touch with his children. He drove round France, trying to find what he had once been, then moved to a squat in Sliedrecht and slept on a mattress on the floor. "I had money in the bank," he says, "but I never touched it. I wanted nothing to do with cycling and the self-centered life that had led to my divorce."

He took up sculpture but then abandoned it when he showed talent at it and there was a risk that it would make him well known again. He lives now in an ordinary housing estate in Dordrecht, in southwest Holland. Some days he glues tiles to walls and floors, other days he fits carpets. In his spare time he works with mentally handicapped children. He now rides a bike again—he belongs to a club in Alkmaar—and he makes appearances with other bygone stars like Jan Janssen—the man whose absence from the world championship unknowingly led to his downfall—and Jo De Roo. "But," he says, "if I could live my life all over again, I'd miss out the cycling bit."

21

HOW TO WIN AGAINST THE ODDS

It doesn't necessarily follow that people who have the guts to win against the odds will also have pleasant personalities. It does on the other hand normally follow that they will have the full complement of limbs, generally recognised as two arms and two legs. Having just one arm when you plan to break the year's mileage record would always be considered a handicap.

In these enlightened times, of course, we no longer ridicule handicapped people. Rather, we admire them while trying at the same time not to patronise. It's a difficult balance to achieve. But when a rider is simply as unpleasant as Walter Greaves, it is impossible. If I tell you that Greaves and his one arm crashed 19 times in the first five days, my bet is that you'll be unsure whether to snigger or not. It's a difficult balance ... you see how hard it is to avoid puns?

The record that Greaves won was, as I said, the year's mileage record. It was dreamed up by the long-defunct British magazine *The Bicycle* back in the 1930s. The record stands at the moment at 75,065 miles or 80,647 miles, according to whether you believe the last man cheated or not. At times, the record has been held by General de Gaulle's chauffeur, an Australian and several Englishmen—but never yet by an American.

The idea of a year-long mileage record was a success from the start. *The Bicycle* wanted a running story to help its sales exactly as *L'Auto* had wanted when it devised the Tour de France. And appropriately, given the historical connection, it was a Frenchman called Marcel Planes who started the list with 34,366 miles. The record then tumbled repeatedly as bike factories signed on riders to prove the superiority of the machines in the heyday of the Thirties. Arthur Humbles just missed 100 miles a day in 1932, then Ossie Nicholson of Australia rode 43,966 and before long the one-armed, vegetarian, teetotal and astonishingly disagreeable Walter Greaves of Bradford took the record to an astonishing 45,383 miles.

There seems no doubt that he did it out of bitterness. Every factory in his home town had blacklisted him as a trouble-making left-winger and he could no longer find work as an engineer. He seemed filled with malice and hatred and the more he showed it the greater the dislike he was shown in return. He just couldn't see the link between his own personality and the way people treated him.

I tried to make a radio documentary about him once. I tracked down people who had known him but only one agreed to talk about the most disagreeable person any of them had ever met. And then, as I tried to arrange to meet, the man changed his mind for fear of what he might say. He would be too embarrassed to express his true feelings about a man both dead and handicapped. That was what creates the confusion in kind and caring people about the fact that Greaves had only one arm or, to be exact, one and a half arms. That, and the absurdity of such a man attempting such a record in the first place, makes it so hard to know how to react to his daily crashes on cobbled roads, tram lines and mountain snow.

But there's no doubt that Greaves was brave. Nicholson, whose record he was challenging, had ridden on tracks and good roads in Australian sunshine, with a manager and a following car. Greaves rode alone and without help on cold and hilly English roads, averaging 120 miles a day by the end of February 1936.

The record attempt was supposed to start on new year's day but Greaves got off to a late start because his bike didn't arrive until January 5. The weather was the worst for years, with snow giving way to rain, hail and gales that blew through March and April. Yet Greaves, on a heavy three-speed bike, was by then averaging 134 miles a day. And that across the bleak and steep roads of the Pennine mountains that run through northern England.

He covered 500 miles in his first five days and fell off 19 times. One day alone he fell off eight times in snow. He spent two weeks in the hospital after a crash with a car and was then forced to raise his average to 160 miles a day to catch up. In mid-September he upped it to

180 miles a day and on December 13 he rode a few laps of the Serpentine lake in Hyde Park in central London to equal the world record in front of a crowd of cyclists. The furthest he'd ridden in one stint was 400 miles and the shortest 65, at which point he'd fallen off again and spent the rest of the day mending his bike.

With the record in the bag, he could relax with a mere 130 miles a day to set his new figures. On December 31, 1936, he stopped outside Bradford town hall with 45,383 miles behind him. He celebrated with a grapefruit. An admirer who offered him champagne was told: "When I want to poison myself, I'll do it with arsenic." That was the kind of man he was, thoroughly miserable even at his happiest moment.

Greaves died in obscurity. He became a blacksmith—with one arm, remember—and took to singing in pubs and clubs. He typically joined a rebel cycling organisation trying to overthrow organised cycling in Britain but seems to have made little mark. He grew into an old man, described by a former acquaintance as "a frail, ragged scarecrow", who ran a café on one of the main roads that led out of Bradford. It's not even certain when he died nor if anyone went to the funeral.

By then his record had long gone. It fell three times in 1937 and twice in 1939. Bernard Bennett was the first to do it. After 45,801 miles in a year he went on for 100,000 miles in 642 days. Yet before he'd ridden the 100,000 he'd lost the year record to a 48-year-old Frenchman, René Menzies. He rode 61,561 miles despite breaking a wrist on ice and riding in a sling made from a racing tire. He, too, went on for 100,000 miles, doing it at the age of 63 during a club ride to the French bike-making city of St-Étienne. Menzies won the Military Cross and the Croix de Guerre in the first world war and became General de Gaulle's chauffeur and valet in the second. He died at 82 while pedalling round Hyde Park Corner in London.

The present record belongs to Tommy Godwin who, with a sponsor, full-time manager and teams of pacers, managed 75,065 miles and rode on to 100,000 miles in 500 days, finishing on May 14, 1940. The Guinness Book of Records briefly listed it as having been beaten by a stocky man called Ken Webb, though. On September 1, 1971—the January 1 start rule had been dropped—he set out from the London newspaper district of Fleet Street to ride 80,560 miles. Nobody believed he could do it, not least because most of his few backers had pulled out.

By November 10, Webb was forced to take a job, ride there from his home near London's Gatwick airport, ride 220 miles after work and then sleep two or three hours before going off to work again. He stopped individuals and called at police stations and post-offices to have his odometer checked. His longest day was 347 miles, once riding 330 without stopping. On August 7, with the help of a few coins sent by a small boy who read of his plight, he lapped St James' Park in London to pass Godwin's record.

His record, and his 100,000 miles in 448 days, are no longer in the record book. The record-keepers began getting letters that cast doubts. Webb denied cheating and he is still bitter. "Among Tommy Godwin's friends, there was a lot of ill-feeling that he had lost his record," he says. "There was talk that I was on drugs, that when I went to bed for a few hours, someone else was clocking up the miles." Doubters followed him during the attempt and then checked if Webb had told the truth. Nothing has ever been proved. But the doubt was too much and he lost his record. So far as I know, nobody has ever attempted it since. But now that you know about it, perhaps the next record-holder could be ... you. Perhaps.

22

HOW TO EMBARRASS A FRENCHMAN

You remember Alphonse Steinès, the man who suffered on the Tourmalet? Well, he was never a man to shirk a task. When Henri Desgrange decided to overcome a little political difficulty and take the Tour into Germany in 1906 for the first time, it was our Alphonse that he sent to Metz to meet the governor. Steinès had to explain that the Tour wanted to come that way as an expression of friendship rather than to cock a snook, because the region that Steinès persuaded Desgrange to cross was the area of France that had been ceded to Germany after defeat in the battle of Sedan, which ended the Franco-Prussian war in 1870.

Just how Desgrange really felt about it, we'll never know. But Steinès was obviously persuasive because both the governor and the politicians in Berlin agreed.

There was some nervousness as the race approached and then crossed the new and obviously sensitive border. The French naturally saw the area as being more French than German and Desgrange's deputy, Victor Breyer, reported that his annexed countrymen had cheered French riders and even French cars as they passed. And the German police, he said, not only behaved impeccably but turned a blind eye to speeding drivers and riders. "You'd never get that from a French policeman," he wrote.

All that was left was a triumphant return to France, covered with glory. France's greatest sporting monument had done what neither politicians nor soldiers had managed, which was to go into the lost territories and emerge in both peace and friendship. These days the race would just sweep across the border with not even a change of police outriders. These days we live in an open Europe where wars are unthinkable and borders are little more than administrative frontiers. But not then. The race had to stop at first the German exit control and then at the barrier that marked the entry back into France. Once more, Breyer reported, the welcome and the technicalities on the German side were impeccable. They were *minutieuses*, said his report back to Paris. The Germans dealt with the race efficiently, with a smile and with the minimum of fuss and the maximum of smartness even though they were having a nap because nobody seemed to have told them the race was coming.

But then, the Tour organisers reported with obvious embarrassment, everything changed as the riders approached the blue, white and red flags of the French border.

"French Customs were the only ones not to give the riders any help at all," said the report, "even when they were coming back into the country. Woken from a deep sleep, obliged to get up in three minutes, the German Customs men appeared before us correctly dressed in new uniforms. At the French border, by contrast, it was simply distressing. Smelly, covered in mud, their clothes patched and discoloured, backs bent, squashed kepis on dirty bodies, the two officials charged with nosing around on behalf of the tax authorities and who represented France revolted us."

The French border men were so slow to get on duty and took so long to cope with their paperwork and all the waiting riders and increasingly frustrated officials and journalists that the judges had to organise a second start. The organising newspaper, *L'Auto*, reported all this with ironic amusement and no little embarrassment. And some anger, too. This was supposed to be a triumphant reoccupation of fallen France. Instead, the old enemy had behaved immaculately while the French had been a shambles.

L'Auto reported the shaming truth at some length—and then cheekily but "very seriously" offered to start a public appeal for money to buy clean clothes for its frontier officials.

23

HOW TO GET A FREE DRINK

I promised you another Wim van Est story. And if you remember how Louis Trousselier managed to get a free meal, here's another free lesson, this time in how to get a free drink.

Times were hard when Wim van Est started racing. People raced on whatever bikes they could afford and often they'd cycle to a race the previous day and spend the night in a farmer's barn. Van Est remembered times when he and his friends would wake at dawn and steal eggs from a hen coop to make themselves breakfast before disappearing. He also remembered his first races, where the *voiture balai*, the pick-up wagon at the back for riders who dropped out, was provided by a local enthusiast. Unfortunately the local enthusiast was the village coal merchant and the only vehicle he could offer was his coal truck, which meant that riders who got left behind when van Est attacked ended up covered in soot as they sat out the rest of the race on the truck. If it rained as well, the sticky streaks of coal dust just completed their misery.

Even when he was a professional in the 1950s he remembered travelling to races abroad, and not by car or plane. "It'd take two, three days in a train, sleeping in the netting racks above the seats where people usually put their suitcases," he recalled. "And if you could, you'd buy a bit of steak from the local butcher and go into a café and ask if they'd cook it for you. If they wouldn't, you'd just eat it raw."

All this moneyless existence extended to training rides. "If you haven't got money then you have to be crafty," he said. "When we went training we had a trick to get ourselves a drink. We'd get to a shop and one of us would lie in the road start groaning in pain as though he'd just fallen off. Someone would always come out of the shop to see what had happened and how he was and my friend in the gutter would ask for a drink and he'd always get one.

"Then he'd get up and we'd start riding again and further up the road we'd share out the drink between us. It solved the problem."

Van Est was the giant of Bordeaux–Paris, a race that's disappeared now but which he won it at its peak, in 1950, 1952 and 1961 when it had enormous glory and significance. The route was long enough to mark on a globe of the world, stretching as it did from the south-western port town of Bordeaux to the French capital. That alone was enough to make it terrifying but the daylight hours were also ridden flat-out behind Derny motorbikes piloted by lugubrious men with spinnaker bellies. A race like that took, er, special preparation.

Van Est remembered: "One of my Belgian team-mates spotted a little box on the front seat of our team manager's car. He could just make out that it held some sort of pills and he asked me if they'd be any good to get him through the race. He said he needed something strong to get him through something as hard as Bordeaux–Paris. I said they were just what he needed and I picked up the box, gave him two of what was inside, and told him to take them a quarter of an hour before the start. And that's what he did. But two kilometers after the start he had to get off his bike because his stomach hurt so much."

At this point van Est erupted into laughter, grabbed my arm with one hand and banged his other on the table as he relived the hilarity of the moment.

"They weren't drugs in the box," he roared. "They were flints for the manager's cigarette lighter."

24

HOW TO PICK THE WRONG MOMENT

In 1965 Jacques Anquetil announced that he was going to ride the Dauphiné Libéré and then go straight to Bordeaux–Paris—Wim van Est's race—and ride that without a night's rest between the two. It wasn't his idea: it was dreamed up by his manager, the flamboyant Raphaël Géminiani, a man with a nose (literally, for it was very large) for publicity.

"You are the Émil Zátopek of cycling," he told Anquetil, referring to the Czech runner who'd won the 5,000 meter, then the 10,000 meter, and then the marathon at the Olympic Games in Helsinki in 1952. It was an event Anquetil remembered because he had been there, riding the team time-trial for France. He took some time to be persuaded but eventually agreed.

Reporters followed the Dauphiné Libéré with more than the usual interest and Raymond Poulidor, who always followed Anquetil like the crocodile following Captain Hook, made a point of attacking him more than usual. He hoped Anquetil would ease up because of the Bordeaux–Paris to follow, but again his strategical sense let him down and he failed. Anquetil won Dauphiné Libéré despite bad weather which he hated and drove from the finish to an airfield and flew from there to Bordeaux in a hired Mystère 20 with just a nap on the way. He then turned up at Quatre Pavilions in the suburbs of Bordeaux where the world's longest single-day road race started. It was the stunt of a lifetime.

The agreement in Bordeaux–Paris was always that riders would stay together through the night and stop at dawn to put on their race clothes before racing on to pick up their Dernys, usually from Châtellerault. It was a tedious part of the race for everyone and often even the officials dozed as they were driven through the night. Reporters were equally bored and not beyond mischief. One year, for instance, the French reporter Pierre Chany borrowed a bike from one of the following mechanics and, having been a reasonable rider in his youth, rode up to the group of well-wrapped professionals and joined in. As he reported later with some glee, he was there for some time before the chief official, Jacques Goddet, came round from his sleep and began counting the riders to see if he'd missed anything. If nothing had happened there would be the same dozen or so starters; if something had happened there'd be fewer, because someone would have gone off the front or off the back. Then he could check the *dossards* and see who was missing. What should never happen is that there'd be *more* riders than there had been at the start.

"Goddet was hopping mad," Chany reported. "He just started rubbing his eyes in disbelief. Then he saw who the extra rider was and started shouting 'Chany, get out of there this minute,' but he was a newspaperman himself and he could always recognise a good story even when it was at his expense."

The year that Anquetil rode, nobody broke away before dawn, as agreed, but unknown to the others the Frenchman Claude Valdois had changed his clothes in the darkness. He attacked when the others stopped to get out of their wet clothes.

"Everybody saw him go and a cry of 'the bastard' went up and it was pandemonium," said Tom Simpson, who was Anquetil's main rival. Anquetil was furious at being duped and considered Simpson in on the deal—which he wasn't—because he and Valdois both rode for the rival Peugeot team. In fact Simpson himself was angry because his manager, Gaston Plaud, had got Valdois to pull off his stunt without taking the polite step of telling Simpson, his star rider.

Anquetil had hired Vin Denson, his team-mate in the Ford team, to protect his interests and he began shouting for him to do something about it, and quickly. Denson recalled: "I jumped after Valdois with my shorts half on, fastening my braces [suspenders], and Stablinski, the other Ford man riding for Anquetil, followed with one sock on and still trying to get his heels in his shoes."

In those days shorts were made of closely woven wool and had genuine chamois inserts. The leather had to be treated with a coating of lanolin, without which it became stiff and unusable, and riders soon found their lanolin and chamois full of grit from the shoes they hadn't had time to take off. They spent the next hour with their hands down the front of their shorts, trying to pick it out as they rode.

Denson had no trouble with gritty shorts but he did have another problem. He'd reckoned on having a pee, his first since Bordeaux. But then Anquetil had shouted for him to chase Valdois and Denson and his bulging bladder had no choice but obey.

Valdois got to Châtellerault first and won the prize for being first to reach his Derny. He set off at 40 mph with Denson behind him, paced by his own Derny. "We were five minutes up," Denson remembers, "when, in agony, I could no longer ignore the insistence of nature and I called to Pleasance, my pacer, to stop. 'You can't stop in Bordeaux–Paris,' he cried, to which I replied 'Watch me!' and I lined up at a tree."

The press and newsreel photographers were grateful for something to film so early in a tedious race and they gathered around Denson, his tree and his lowered shorts, joined by journalists, officials, the embarrassed and despairing Pleasance, several passers-by, and a wintertime gravedigger called Bernard Stoops who worked each summer as a *soigneur*, a cross between a witch doctor and soothsayer akin to old-time boxing seconds whose job it was to get Denson through the race.

The little crowd gave Denson an attack of nerves, which did nothing for his plumbing, pounded as it was by riding through the rain all night. For five minutes he stood hopelessly by his tree as the cameras whirred and the crowd cheered him on like a racehorse. Other riders began droning past behind their pacers. And then along came Anquetil, the very man whom Denson had been engaged to protect. To Denson's horror, Anquetil had become locked in the very 350 km battle with Simpson that he was supposed to prevent.

Now thoroughly miserable and still unsatisfied, Denson pulled up his shorts and set off once more, not only behind Pleasance but now also behind Anquetil. But that bladder was still bursting. Fifty kilometers later he stopped again and the same delighted reporters circled him once more, joined by Pleasance and Stoops but a fresh set of onlookers.

"This time I had an unrewarding three minutes," Denson recalled with a mix of agony and amusement, "until the *soigneur* [Stoops] came up and did the trick with the aid of hot coffee on a sponge."

I have no idea what Anquetil said to Denson when they next met. The Frenchman had turned to Jean Stablinski to do the job instead and he and Anquetil-the-strategist took turns in attacking Simpson so that the Englishman had to respond to both and wear himself out. Eventually Simpson cracked and Anquetil won by getting clear in the final kilometers. He had to be taken straight to the hospital, exhausted and with first signs of a lung infection after pulling off his astonishing double. Stablinski came second and Simpson came third and had to be helped off his bike. Denson probably just went into hiding.

25

HOW TO RACE AGAINST THE IMPOSSIBLE

In the great days, Bordeaux–Paris was ridden behind Derny motorbikes, named after the family in Paris that made them as an improvement on the heavy belt-driven machines used on the track and sometimes on the road. Originally, though, the race was run behind first human pacers and then behind cars.

The thing to remember is that cycling and driving haven't always been as separate as they are now. The enthusiasm was for being on the road, for not being on a horse or on foot. Many bike-makers made cars and motorcycles and many early cyclists saw the excitement of the new bicycle in the way that some people are excited these days by fast cars. And, in just the same way, they drifted on to cars and abandoned bicycles when they sensed that was the way that excitement lay.

Pacing in cycling was accepted, even wanted, as the way to make riders race as fast as possible. In fact one of the criticisms of the first Tour de France was that pacers were allowed only on the final stage to Paris. The race would be tediously slow, the doubters forecast. For that reason nobody thought it very odd when riders in the 1897 Bordeaux–Paris tucked in behind giant cars with heavy spoked wheels, big square hoods and with their drivers perched high behind flat driving wheels, sitting outside in heavy overcoats, caps and giant goggles.

At first cars appeared only in the closing hours, especially beyond the city of Tours. But the following year, 1898, riders rode behind them all the way from Bordeaux. That certainly added spectacle because the cars were huge and noisy, billowing exhaust and creating great desert storms of dust on the unsurfaced roads. But the danger was enormous. The riders could see nothing but the back of their car, for hours on end, they could shout nearly nothing to their helpers above the noise, and they rarely had worthwhile brakes to stop them in time if the car broke down in a skid, which wasn't rare.

Fortunately, given the danger, teams of cars and riders rarely raced side by side. They were separated by several minutes, although now and then one team would try to pass another, which must have looked like stagecoaches and galloping horses attempting to outrace each other. The danger of the attempt made it undesirable, drivers not being averse to filling as much of the road as they could and even zigzagging to discourage overtaking. If that failed and a team was overtaken, it would have to repeat the maneuver to get back in front.

That and the sheer wish to win was on the mind of the Frenchman Constant Huret, whose name lived on for a century as a brand of derailleurs, when he was wrapped up in a personal battle in 1899 with the giant German Tour de France rider, Josef Fischer. Huret's driver was pacing him through the night at the fastest speed he thought his rider could manage when he glanced in his mirror and to his astonishment saw Huret gesturing to him to go faster.

The driver, surprised but willing, pressed the accelerator a little harder and the car lurched forward. Huret got out of the saddle and turned his single gear a little faster in response. But then again he shouted for the driver to go faster. Because, reflected in the back of the big flat windshield, he could see what his driver couldn't: the headlights of Fischer's own pacer coming up behind.

Once more the driver went faster and this time he demanded to know why. Huret shouted Fischer's name, pointed over his shoulder, and yelled "*Plus vite! Plus vite!*" The driver, worried now, pushed his car as fast as it would go. The speedometer crept from 45 to beyond 50 km/h, the engine roared, the hard wheels bounced on the bumpy, dusty road and the near-direct steering was almost out of control. The driver feared a bend in the road, a sudden reason to change direction, an emergency stop; he knew he wouldn't be able to cope. The car would plunge into a ditch and both driver and rider could be killed. And yet once more Huret shouted for more speed.

Desperately worried now, the driver snatched a look over his shoulder to see for himself where Fischer was, to marvel at how the German's pacer could cope with speeds and roads that were beyond him. But other than Huret, the road was empty, just unrelenting blackness. There was nothing there but the dust that he and Huret had created.

So the driver slowed a little, relieved that the pressure and danger were off, and then slowed again. Huret, though exhausted, was determined and angry. He began to swear at his driver, telling him he could see the lights of Fischer's car. Was the man crazy? Could he not see for himself? What did he think he was being paid for? There was a race to win, a rival to beat.

The driver argued in return and finally persuaded Huret to look behind himself as well. And Huret, to his amazement, also saw the road was empty. Nobody could have followed at that crazy speed and in fact nobody had tried to. Unknown to both men, Fischer had slowed and was way, way behind them.

It was at this point that Huret felt extremely, extremely stupid. He had seen Fischer's headlights in the windshield, he said, mystified. There was no doubt about it: the German had been there, and not only there but closing. The driver probably smiled then as he realised the truth. He raised a gloved hand and pointed into the night sky. Huret looked round and upwards. Behind them, a third of the way above the horizon, was a large and cloudless moon. It was that that had reflected in the windshield, that which Huret had taken for Fischer's headlights.

For hours, at speeds that risked both men's lives, they had been racing the moon.

The footnote, by the way, is that Fischer had his revenge the following year and that after that the organisers abandoned cars and went back to pacing by humans. Just as well, really.

26

HOW TO GO INTO THE FUTURE—LYING DOWN

There have been many ideas of which we've never heard again, and some that come round time and again. The puncture-proof tire is one. It was being promoted as long ago as 1905 when spectators and perhaps even riders were still going on with an early tradition of scattering nails in the path of rivals. That led an inventor called Cavalade to demonstrate a puncture-proof tire in the Café Sion during the Tour's rest day at Toulouse.

A reporter wrote: "Dortignacq got on the inventor's bicycle, rode quickly, then slowly, jumped on the pedals, balanced on the nails and jumped the bike on to them. There was no puncture, the nails falling from the tires at the first turn ... All the Tour riders tried it ... The bike was convincing and the riders warmly thanked M. Cavalade, who put the invention at their disposition, without obligation, for the stages still to come."

I've no idea whether the riders went as far as using the invention. I suspect they didn't or we'd still know about it. But the idea never goes away. Go to any bike show and you can still see the same idea being promoted—and rejected. The last time I saw it was when a Dutch company had rigged up a back wheel which it invited show-visitors to ride repeatedly through a bed of broken glass. Most people passed by with no more than a world-weary glance.

A few ideas have stayed, though, even though they weren't popular at the time and remain banned in conventional races now. Take the idea of the Frenchman Charles Mochet, for instance. It sounds crazy now but he used to make and sell full-scale pedal cars, complete with a steering wheel and a seat for a passenger. If you couldn't afford a real car, as many couldn't in the years between the wars, you could at least look as though you could. Up to a point; you had to pedal rather than start up a motor and, although they went surprisingly fast, their stability didn't match their performance and they were prone to tumble over on corners.

Most bike makers in history have gone on to make cars but Mochet went the other way. He split his vélocar down the middle and turned it into a single-seat bike. The wheels were just 50 cm across, which put the rider very close to the ground. As Mochet explained, there was no point in making them larger because there was no chance of the pedals hitting the ground on corners. They also made the rider more aerodynamic.

To make that wind-cheating even better, he put the rider horizontal, sitting on a proper seat with a back rest and with his legs stretched out in front of him. The pedals were ahead of the rest of the bike and turned a chainring linked to the back wheel by a long chain. The handlebars stretched back from the front wheel to where the rider could reach them. In other words, eight decades ago Mochet had invented what many now think is a recent invention: the recumbent or horizontal bicycle.

His interest wasn't only racing. He was more keen to show that his bike could be used for everyday riding and even for touring with luggage. But not unless he could interest people in racing could he publicise and prove his machine's advantages. He persuaded the French professional Henri Lemoine to give it a go. Lemoine had come second in the 1930 Critérium des As in Paris and was therefore a name worth interesting. He opted to try the vélocar on the circuit that the race used at Longchamp.

"Believe me," Mochet told him, "you'll go faster than on your ordinary bike." He pointed out the gear far higher than an ordinary rider would use but which Lemoine could turn with ease, he said, because he could make his legs stronger by pushing back against the back of the seat. Lemoine set off and was quickly impressed. He passed other riders out training, and they watched him in astonishment and then tried but failed to slide into his slipstream. But there was no slipstream: Lemoine was too near the ground and one by one the other riders dropped off exhausted.

Mochet wanted Lemoine to ride in races but the rider declined. Yes, the bike was good but, no, he wasn't prepared to be ridiculed. So Mochet turned to a lesser rider, Francis Faure, whose brother Benoît was one of the star climbers of the Tour de France. Faure agreed to ride on the Vélodrome d'Hiver, Paris's indoor track. He soon realised that Lemoine had been right about the ridicule. "Ah, monsieur, needs to lie down because he's tired?", the other riders laughed as he trundled round the wooden banking. But their smiles died when Faure broke short-distance records set by Lucien Michard and then the 50 km time of Maurice Richard, the world hour-record holder.

He and Mochet were delighted. They went to the Union Vélocipédique Française, the French national body, and asked it to accept the records. But the federation declined, worried even before Mochet came knocking on their door that things had taken a bad turn. The officials refused.

"Show us where the rules say Faure can't ride on such a machine," Mochet protested, and French officialdom looked and admitted it couldn't find any reason to exclude him. But there is more than one way to deal with a situation if you're determined and the UVF said that in the absence of rules, its only course was to write some. It couldn't deny Faure his records but instead it created a "special bikes" section and put them in there.

In October 1932 Mochet appealed to the world body, the UCI. Officials there had the same worries. They hadn't liked the way things had gone back in the days of people like the Swiss rider, Oscar Egg, who in 1914 beat Marcel Berthet's hour record of 41.520 km and reset it at 44.247 km. He did it on a bike with a streamlined fairing, which became known as *l'œuf d'Oscar* in French and as Oscar's Egg in English. That, the UCI had long decided, had gone altogether too fast and there'd be a time when races became just too dangerous because of the speed. And just think of the carnage if all that fairing got tangled up in somebody else's bike … Indeed, the Dutch world champion Piet Dickentman and the European champion, Arthur Stellbrink from Berlin, did crash and Dickentman died. The UCI changed the rules in 1914. It banned all streamlining, which is still the position today.

Mochet protested, saying his bike wasn't streamlined; Egg's bike had had the streamlining but on the vélocar only the rider was streamlined, and that broke no rules. But the UCI, like the UVF, was having none of it. If there were no rules, then it too would write some. And so, also to this day, there are rules on the size of wheels, where the saddle has to be in relation to the frame and the length and width of a bicycle. And more rules besides.

Faure then broke the world hour record on July 7, 1933 and the row continued. Some countries saw the vélocar as the future of cycling, others refused to accept it as a bike. Bubbling beneath the row was a feeling that a little rider like Faure (he was little in both size and achievement) had no right to be any sort of champion or record holder. Clearly it was the bike that had done it.

Seven decades later, the UCI came to the same conclusion again and effectively dismissed all the hour records set since Eddy Merckx in Mexico in 1972. All the others, it summarised, had been helped as much by better bikes as better riders. In that time the record had moved from the Belgian rider's 49.431 km to the 56.375 km of Chris Boardman in 1996. An improvement which had taken only 24 years on so-called "funny" bikes had taken 59 years on a conventional machine. That, the UCI argued, was too great an improvement to be due to increased fitness alone.

The last I heard of the Mochet vélocar was that it was in the bike museum at Einbeck, Germany. But the legend lives on in what is now called Human-Powered Vehicle racing, a deliberately vague name that demonstrates that, unlike in the world of the UCI, anything goes so long as only a human moves it.

27

HOW TO ENTER THE TOUR DE FRANCE (1)

Francis Faure, as I said, was the brother of Benoît, the king of the *touristes-routiers.* Years back, instead of just reading about the Tour, you could enter it. Just like that. There weren't enough teams so, provided you didn't cause Henri Desgrange any extra work, you could join in.

These privateers went under various names but the most popular was *touriste-routier.* They were a tough bunch. They had no team manager, no soigneur, no mechanic, nobody even to buy train tickets. After each stage they rode round town with a suitcase on their handlebars to find a cheap hotel. If there was nowhere cheap enough, they slept in barns or on benches. Next morning they put their bags on the train to the next stage town and joined in with the race.

Hardship was no stranger to any of them. Jules Deloffre would race for 10 hours and then perform acrobatic tricks in the street, standing upside down on borrowed chairs. Then he would take his cap round the crowd to raise the centimes for his hotel. And yet he finished the Tour seven times between 1908 and 1921 and only twice outside the first two dozen.

The most fondly remembered *touriste-routier* was Benoît Faure. In 1930 he broke away between Pau and Luchon in the Pyrenees, rode over the Aubisque and then the Soulor and had five minutes' lead at the top of the Tourmalet. He was too light for the rutted and unmade road of the descent, though, and Alfredo Binda and the rising star André Leducq caught him as he bounced uncomfortably from one hole to the next. Binda won the stage, Leducq became *maillot jaune* and Faure came fifth.

Desgrange was impressed by this little buccaneer and was so determined to get the brilliant little climber into proper team that he paid his fare to Paris to lecture him on joining Alcyon, the top team of the day. But Faure stuck with his personal backer, Le Cheminot ("The Railwayman"), for half what Alcyon was offering.

"I'd been a *touriste-routier*, a loner, too long," he said. "I wasn't a good team man and I envied the freedom of riders without any obligation." On the one occasion he was tempted into the French team to ride for Antonin Magne against Italy, "I went after a 2,000-franc prime and started a rare old battle in which the Italians happily joined in. They took the first three places. Magne was mad with me, the whole team too, but maddest of all was Henri Desgrange. He'd written a book called *Head and Legs*. A rider needed both, he said. But I, Benoît, just stumbled along on my legs."

28

HOW TO ENTER THE TOUR DE FRANCE (2)

If Benoît Faure was the king of the *touristes-routiers,* then Jules Banino comes close to Jules Deloffre for being the most colourful. Banino was a policeman from the Mediterranean coast who rode the Tour in his vacations. Policemen are usually well-ordered and unexciting people, which is what you want for a murder investigation or in someone administering a disaster. But Banino was game for anything. No challenge, no wild adventure was too much for him. If there wasn't a bike race, there'd be something else. Just the slightest mention of a slippery-pole competition or a holding-your-breath-underwater contest and he'd be there.

Roger Dries says in *Le Tour de France de Chez Nous*: "You saw him in all the sports events ever organised. There was a swimming meeting? He'd be the first to turn up, perched on his bike, and he'd dive into the sea and take part. A pole-climbing contest? Banino would be there. He once even took on the same wager as the Count of Monte Cristo [hero of the book by Alexandre Dumas], tying himself in a sack and being thrown into the Mediterranean, at Tabau-Capeu. He almost drowned. He had to be pulled out in a hurry and he was hardly breathing when they got to him."

If you're ever asked to name the Tour's oldest rider, Banino is the man. He was 51 when he rode in 1924, which tells you something of the man's spirit of adventure. He didn't finish then or in 1923 because the unmade roads were so bad that he was blinded by clouds of dust and finished outside the time limit. Much of the dust was thrown up by the organisers' cars but Henri Desgrange had no sympathy and kicked Banino out of the race.

In 1924 that meant he had to get home to Nice. So that night, with the toughness and bizarre stupidity of his kind, he set off on his bike, riding in the dark with the coincidence that the next day's stage was starting that same night and also going towards Nice.

Many of the longest stages in those days started early in the morning and it was common for riders to stay together and leave the attacks until daylight. But that morning the leaders were cracking along when they were horrified to hear that a rider was ahead of them. The stars looked around, saw that all the *gros bras* were still there and concluded that they were being shown up by an also-ran. There was hurt pride in that and they grew angry. They accelerated to 35 km/h on the bumpy and stone-strewn roads and dropped down hills at 50. Finally, in the headlights of cars lighting their way, they spotted a lone figure with its legs twirling. This was no farmer heading for his fields. This was a *coureur*, a *coursier*.

"Who are you?" they demanded when they pulled up alongside.

"I'm Jules Banino, an amateur. I'm just riding home at my own pace."

The expression "my own pace" wasn't, perhaps, well-chosen. The stars, thinking he was in the race, had just spent an hour chasing hard to catch him, on roads that threatened both man and bike. It turned out they had been humbled by not just "an amateur" but by a man simply riding home. Ottavio Bottechia, a mild-mannered, sullen Italian with wing-nut ears who was leading the Tour, took especial offence and began thumping him. That inspired the others to join in and in the end Jean Alavoine gave Banino such a kick that he tumbled into a ditch.

That ought to have been enough misfortune for one night. Unfortunately, a bunch of Alavoine's supporters happened to be standing by the roadside at that moment. Not having seen everything that had happened, they assumed their man was defending himself rather than just giving Banino a good kicking. Casting the victim as the villain, and ignoring the man's protests, they rounded on him as he lay in his ditch and began hitting him with sticks. It took several hours before he'd recovered enough to complete his ride home.

29

HOW TO OVERCOME TRAGEDY

Banino's suffering, though, was nothing compared to that of the Frenchman Honoré Barthélemy. He crashed face-first into the ground on the stage to Aix-en-Provence of the Tour de France in 1920. He climbed back on his bike, groggy and bleeding, and started wobbling down the road. His eyes were blurred, his arms hurt terribly, and his back was in such pain that he was forced to turn his handlebars up the other way so he would no longer have to bend.

Then an awful truth came to him: his eyes weren't blurred at all. He had a concussion, yes, and that made everything fuzzy. But to his horror he realised he had gone blind in one eye. The crash had pushed a flint into it and in his pain and misery he hadn't realised.

These days he would have been taken to the hospital long before getting back on his bike. But what makes this the ultimate story of cycling heroism is that Barthélemy finished not only the stage but the Tour itself, coming eighth despite his semi-blindness and constant pain. He had also broken a shoulder and dislocated a wrist and yet he rode on. He was the hero of the race and when he reached the finish at the Parc des Princes, crowds ran on to the track to carry him in triumph.

Nothing could stop him. When the Tour finished he bought himself a glass eye and carried on racing. The eyeball looked fine in ordinary life and even when he was racing on good roads. But the dust of the hot summers in southern France gave him dreadful problems because, not being a real eye, it didn't water properly. When life got too tough, he would sit upright, take his hands off the bars, press the eye from of its socket, wrap it up in a handkerchief and put it in his pocket. Then he'd fill the hole with cotton wool. If he didn't, it would fester.

"It makes no difference to the view but it's softer and I always like a bit of pampering," he used to say with irony.

The journalist Albert Londres spotted him by the roadside in the 1924 Tour, on an epic 412 km stage from Brest to Les Sables d'Olonne. He recorded: "Another rider has stopped by the side of the road; he's not repairing his machine but his face. He's got one real eye and one glass one. He takes the eye out to wipe it. 'I've only had it four months; I'm not used to it.' He tapped the socket. 'It's got pus in it.'

"'You in pain?'

"'No, but my brain's leaking.'"

Unfortunately the glass eye often fell out. Barthélemy was more than once reduced to getting down on his knees at the finish to see where it had rolled. "I don't know why I carry on racing," he complained. "I win my prizes and then I have to spend them all on buying new glass eyes for the ones I lose in races."

He rode the Tour eight times between 1919 and 1927 and won five stages, coming third overall in 1921. He died in May 1964, a forgotten hero of the days when men didn't let fear get in the way of their dreams.

30

HOW TO RIDE LIKE AN EXPRESS

The first Tour de France went the way it did not because Henri Desgrange thought it the best available course but because the trains also went that way. The organisers looked for cities that had big bike tracks—it would be there that the most spectators would be attracted because they already knew about cycle-racing—then checked the train timetable to be sure that they were accessible in the days when the roads were fine for cyclists and horses but too hard for rigid, bone-shattering and mechanically unreliable cars.

The man who thought of the Tour, Géo Lefèvre, also became its roving official, judge and reporter. Luckily he was one of the best riders of his club on the outskirts of Paris, so he could see the riders away at the start of the day and then ride to the nearest station and catch a train or a series of trains to the finish.

Nobody knew whether the schedule would work because nobody knew how fast the riders would go. In fact Lefèvre arrived at the first finish at Lyon after the winner, Maurice Garin. The little man was waiting for him with a cigarette dangling from his lips. Lefèvre, not being entirely stupid, made the best of his blunder and tried to disguise it from Henri Desgrange, who hadn't been confident enough of his own race to follow it, by boasting: "The riders are going even faster than the train."

That was 1903. Lefèvre would have known, therefore, about Charlie Murphy and the date of June 30, 1899. It was then that Murphy, a boastful kid from Brooklyn, New York, achieved what was considered the impossible: to ride a mile in a minute, faster than any human before him. And he did it behind a train, persuading a railway company to board in a couple of miles of track and run a train so he could sit in its smoke and smut and ride at 60 mph. It took him 57.8 seconds to ride a mile.

Murphy did it because he had got into an argument about how fast a cyclist could go. He recalled: "My answer was that there was no limit to the speed of a bicycle rider, that speed depended largely upon the bicycle, gears, tracks and pacemaker. I declared there was not a locomotive built which could get away from me. The more people laughed, the more determined I became to accomplish the feat. I figured that the fast-moving locomotive would expel the air to such an extent that I could follow in the vacuum behind."

To understand this, you need a little physics. A vacuum is not the same thing as suction. It will not suck you along, Murphy insisted. Freewheel and the train will move away, whereas if there was suction you wouldn't have needed to pedal in the first place. All the train would do, he said, was reduce the air in front of him and therefore its resistance to his progress.

Murphy had already ridden a mile in 37 seconds on a home-trainer. So, he reasoned, with a big enough shield he could go as fast as he liked. The fastest thing on earth in 1899 was a train. Ultimate cycling speed records were all but unknown because little went fast enough for high-speed pacing. The magic speed was a mile in a minute and even trains couldn't dependably do it.

"By chance," Murphy said, "I met Hal Fullerton, special agent of the Long Island Railroad at Howes Roadhouse. I pointed out that an exhibition of that kind would prove to the world that the Long Island Railroad had just as good rolling stock, roadbeds and employees as any other road in the world."

The two men signed a contract within 48 hours. James E. Sullivan, secretary of the American Athletic Union, was appointed to be referee and there were five timekeepers. Reporters came from all over the country. They arrived in Babylon, New Jersey, at 5 PM on June 21, 1899, mounted the train and watched.

Murphy told Sam Booth, the driver of locomotive 39, to go as fast as he could and hold it. Then he dressed in his "racing togs", as he called his cycling clothes, and climbed on to his Tribune bike with its giant gear. Fullerton had spread a two-mile carpet of boards between the rails from Babylon to Farmingdale, then added side-wings and a small roof to the observation platform at the back of the last carriage.

Murphy didn't expect the train to move away quite so fast up the slight slope but he stayed in the middle of the planks and within inches of the beam and crossbar that was his bumper on the observation platform below the judges, dignitaries and timekeepers. He clocked 16.4 seconds for the first quarter-mile, 33.6 for the half, 49.2 for the three-quarters and the mile in 1:08. He dropped back 70 yards into eddies of wind that threw him about "as if I were a piece of paper." He had gone too slowly.

Fullerton, who'd hoped to impress the world, was embarrassed to find his locomotive wasn't fast enough. Six times it failed to get to 60 mph, the mile in a minute. He replaced it with his heaviest and fastest locomotive but Murphy then was forced to ride a wave as the engine's weight made the wooden track sink and rise as it passed over the joints of the rails. Even so, he said he'd try it and as the train moved away he held the railing of the observation platform until he'd got his bike rolling. Fullerton then asked if he was all right, Murphy nodded that he was and Fullerton told driver Booth to open the regulator. The ride into history had started.

"With eyes glued upon the vertical strip of white on back of the car … I experienced an entirely different feeling compared with my previous ride," Murphy recalled. "The officials knew that there was something wrong, that I was labouring under great difficulties. I could not understand the violent vibration in the track, as though I was riding over an undulation instead of level track; feeling hot missiles striking my face and body. I learned afterwards it was burning rubber from under the car.

"Within five seconds the rate of speed was terrific; I was riding in a maelstrom of swirling dust, hot cinders, paper and other particles of matter. The whipsaw feeling through a veritable storm of fire became harder every second." Then he started losing ground. An official called Fred Burns shouted through a megaphone to ask what was wrong. Murphy looked up to answer and immediately fell back 15 meters. Instead of setting a record, he was fighting to stay in touch.

"I could feel myself getting weaker every second. I saw ridicule, contempt, disgrace and a lifetime dream gone up in smoke. I saw the agonised faces, yelling, holding out stretched hands as if they would like to get hold of or assist me somehow. The half-mile passed in 29.4 seconds and the ride was rescued.

"Wobbling to and fro, but still gaining, the dust, the odour of burning rubber … The car was crowded with men who had been used to seeing any and all things that were dangerous, but the howling and screaming of sturdy officials and newspaper men from all over the United States that stood on the platform put all on edge. Suddenly, three-quarters was passed in 43⁴/₅ seconds."

Murphy was still five meters back.

"I expected to go off the track, travelling faster than the train, with the terrible storm of dust, pebbles, hot rubber and cinders. I looked up blankly. It was getting to a point where I could expect anything."

A waving Stars and Stripes flashed past the edge of his eye. He had finished. But now Murphy was riding faster than the train, still catching it. Driver Booth, on the other hand, had also seen the flag and he'd shut off steam. Murphy crashed into the observation platform. The bike tipped up and officials grabbed for him. Murphy let go of the handlebars and grasped an upright beam. For a moment he hung there until Fullerton caught one arm and a man called Joseph H. Cummin the other and they pulled both Murphy and his bike to safety.

"I lay motionless, face down, on the platform. I was all in. I was half-carried to a cot at the end of the car; the roar of the train was challenged by hysterical yells. Grown men hugged and kissed each other. One man fainted and another went into hysterics, while I remained speechless on my back, ashen in colour and sore all over," Murphy said. Officials pulled off his jersey for a doctor, McMunn Holly, to examine him. They didn't realise that hot rubber and cinders had burnt through the jersey and that, as they pulled, they were pulling away flesh as well.

Booth, the giant, brown-eyed driver, came back through the train. He'd seen Murphy drop back on the first ride and had expected him to do the same on the second. But this time Murphy hadn't eased back when he shut off steam at the end of the wooden track, so he feared he'd piled into the unprotected sleepers between the rails and crashed. He gasped in shock when he saw Murphy on his cot: he thought he was dead.

And many people *were* shocked. Sullivan, the referee, said he'd never take part in an event of that kind again, even if it made cycling famous for a century. Murphy, on the other hand, cashed in on his fame and became one of 600 professionals on the American circuit. He then joined the New York police. He boasted of being the first policeman in the world to fly an aeroplane, and the first in New York to ride a motorcycle in uniform. In fact, to be honest, he just never stopped boasting.

He died on February 17, 1950, aged 79. In 2000 Farmingdale held a Mile-A-Minute celebration. The *Farmingdale Post* described him as "one of the men who added a bright spot of colour to Farmingdale history."

31

HOW TO DESCEND A MOUNTAIN … painfully

Next time you climb the Soulor and Aubisque, the twin passes that lie across the valley from the Tourmalet, look out for a small plaque fastened to the roadside. It marks, says Karel Hubert, the Dutch businessmen who put it there, the start of his country's Tour history. It also marks the site of our last and most dramatic Wim van Est story.

In 1951, van Est became the first Dutchman to wear the yellow jersey. At home in St-Willebrord, sitting by a table with a heavy cloth across it, he told the story a millionth time but as if it were the first. It never ceased to amaze and amuse him.

"The day I got the *gele trui*, I was away with a group of 13, 14 riders," he said. "And there was a really fast rider with us, Caput the Frenchman, a good sprinter. He attacked a kilometer from the line but we got him back. But when we got to the track, it was an ash track, a horse-racing track. Well, on a track like that I was unbeatable. I'd raced on that sort of finish so often before … Coppi, Kübler … that I was unbeatable. And I won and took the yellow jersey.

"Well, the next day there were several cols, on the stage from Dax to Tarbes. The Tourmalet was one, and then the Aubisque. There were nine or ten men away and we were gritting our teeth to get them back, and then in the first bend of the descent, there was just Ockers [the Belgian rider Stan Ockers, who died in a crash at Antwerp track] and Coppi, a few hundred meters in front of us.

"Well, that first bend was wet, slippery from the snow. And there were sharp stones on the road that the cars had kicked up, and my front wheel hit them and I went over. There was a drop of 700 meters. They've built a barrier round it now but then there was nothing to stop your going over. I fell 20 meters, rolling and rolling and rolling. My feet had come out of the straps, my bike had disappeared, and there was a little flat area, the only one that's there, no bigger than the seat of a chair, and I landed on my backside. A meter to the left or right and I'd have dropped on to solid stone, six or seven hundred meters down.

"My ankles were all hurt, my elbows were *kaput*, I was all bruised and shaken up and I didn't know where I was, but nothing was broken. I just lay there. And the other riders were going by, I could see. And then right at the top I could make out my team-mate, Gerrit Peeters, looking down at me.

"'You looked just like a buttercup down there', he told me afterwards, with the yellow jersey on, you know."

It didn't take long for help to arrive. The team car was driven by Kees Pellenaars, the former Dutch champion who at that time was the one manager of any repute in Holland. In the years when Pellenaars couldn't find a sponsor, there was no real Dutch professional team and the country's best riders had to look abroad for work.

Pellenaars was following his team and race leader as closely as he could and quickly realised what had happened. The other contenders for victory, of course, didn't know where van Est was. They assumed that he was still up near the front and started a hellish chase after a man they could never have guessed was sitting on a tiny mountain ledge 20 meters below them.

Pellenaars stopped his car and peered down the slope. Van Est signalled weakly that he was still alive and not in too bad a shape for a man who had fallen off a mountain and Pellenaars returned to the team car. It was equipped for many eventualities but all of them concerned with cycling. None of the immediate possibilities suggested a link with mountaineering.

Then an idea struck him. He rummaged in the back and pulled out a tow rope, which in those days many drivers carried. He threw it towards van Est but the end dangled well short. And then he was forced to innovate.

"They got 40 sew-ups," van Est said, "knotted them together, tied them to the tow rope and threw it down to me. It was all the tires that

Pellenaars had for the team. By the time they'd tugged me up, they were all stretched and they wouldn't stay on the wheels any more. Forty tires!"

There's a remarkable sequence of pictures which show van Est deep in the ravine, so small that he has to be circled to identify him in the mass of rocks and flecks of snow. His yellow jersey is dirty. It has old-fashioned collars and round it is wrapped the spare tire that riders knotted across their shoulders in those days. Helpers have started to crawl down to him, a man in what looks like a suit and tie and another possibly in overalls and a cotton cap.

They are checking van Est, perhaps for broken bones, and then he starts to climb almost on hands and knees, grasping the tufts of wiry grass that have survived at that altitude. Finally comes the vertical face, maybe 15 meters high, over which he plunged. It is rock with vertical crevices but no ledges on which to plant a foot. By now he is within the length of the tow rope and the last pictures show it taut and diagonal as van Est wonders where to put his leather cycling shoes ready to join the small crowd at the top. Somehow he makes it.

"I wanted to get on my bike and start riding again," he said. "One of the journalists gave me a flask of cognac, and I was saying 'I want to go on.' But I couldn't. Pellenaars stopped the whole team. 'We'll be back next year,' he said. It was good publicity. I got home and the whole neighbourhood was out to greet me."

In the pictures, you can just make out that van Est is wearing a wristwatch above his primitive leather mitts. The company that made it certainly saw it. Van Est got a call from Pontiac's man in Switzerland and days later advertisements appeared in newspapers all over Europe. Beside a picture of a smiling and relieved van Est was the boast: "My heart stopped … but not my Pontiac."

A professional to the end.

32

HOW TO HAVE A RIDE ON THE TRAIN

Trains play a big role in bike racing. These days it happens only when a crossing gate splits the chase from the break or when riders are shipped between towns during the Tour de France or other stage races. In 1903, though, the route of the first Tour was planned along train lines that officials could use to follow their race; a few years later the buccaneering private entrants, the *touristes-routiers*, put their luggage on to trains because they had no team cars to carry it.

There are suspicions that riders in 1904 expanded the concept of cycle-racing to include taking a train part of the way themselves, and in 1906 they certainly did: Maurice Carrère, Henri Gauban and Gaston Tuvache all took a short cut by train only to emerge from the station to find startled Tour officials studying a map at the exit. They suffered the consequences.

Sometimes, though, you couldn't blame riders if they got fed up with riding. In 1905 vandals and possibly even other riders once more scattered nails on the road of the Tour to sabotage it. Henri Desgrange had only narrowly been persuaded to run the race again after the scandals and multiple disqualifications of the previous year, when he'd written that the Tour had been killed "by the passions it has aroused." It was just too much when saboteurs scattered 275 pounds of nails on the first stage of 1905. It later emerged that the nails had been bought all at the same time at a single shop in Paris and Desgrange, rightly suspecting organised wreckers, wanted to cancel the race. Only one rider survived that day without puncturing. Others struggled on after numerous punctures or caught the train to get to the finish.

Having been persuaded against cancelling the race, Desgrange wanted to eliminate all but the 15 who finished within the time limit. Then the riders went on strike to persuade him to keep in anybody who reached the finish however late they'd got there.

The gesture came too late for Lucien Petit-Breton, though. He was one of the stars of the race and the man who that year broke the world hour record. He had run out of tires and he had felt so fed up that he headed for the nearest station. There he bought a ticket for Paris and an escape from the ridiculous misery not only that Desgrange was inflicting with his infernal race but the disastrous interference of outsiders. He fumed angrily all the way to the station and sat on the platform in a great smoking temper of resentment as he waited for his train.

The trip to Paris took several hours and by then, as so often, he had had time to reflect and regret. Petit-Breton wasn't at all so sure he really did want to abandon the Tour. He was, after all, a racing cyclist. It was what he did. His job. There was nothing else and he began to realise it. And then something odd happened. As he got out of the train in Paris, the first man he saw on the platform was Robert Coquelle, a journalist, who said with some astonishment, "I thought you were riding the Tour de France."

Petit-Breton explained all that had happened, how he was angry with the way the race had been ruined but also that he wished he hadn't been so hasty. Coquelle listened with sympathy and also with the awareness that he had a heck of a story for the following morning's paper. Then he said, "Go back to the Tour. Don't worry, I know Desgrange; he'll let you restart."

Coquelle was hardly in a position to make a promise because he was as far from the race as Petit-Breton was and even less connected. But sometimes all you need to hear are the words you need to hear and Petit-Breton walked straight from the train to the ticket office, bought himself a ticket to Nancy and next morning he stepped out of the Orient-Express at Nancy and rode to the start. There he reported for duty as usual. Coquelle had been right; Desgrange's notorious temper had subdued and instead of sending Petit-Breton off on yet another train journey, he docked him 70 points—the Tour was decided on points rather than time—which put him last on the stage but kept him in the race.

He finished the Tour, too, coming fifth.

The same didn't go for the wonderfully named Hippolyte Pagie, though. An official standing by Montelimar station on the second stage of the 1903 Tour was astonished to see him sweaty and dust-streaked on the platform, carrying his bike on his shoulder. He was all the more startled because Pagie, like Petit-Breton, was no also-ran; he was second to Maurice Garin, the eventual winner, but he had lost time in a crash 20 km down the road at Loriol and he had despaired of mending his bike. That was why he was carrying it. He was also cut and bleeding.

The official approached him and asked what was happening.

"I've had enough," Pagie said. "I'm quitting."

"But you can't," the official protested. "You must press on."

Pagie, too weary to argue, shrugged and rode 10 km back towards Loriol. There he turned and rode back to Montelimar, in that way repaying the 20 km he owed the race. He started again next day. But neither his injuries nor his morale had improved and he abandoned.

33

HOW TO ORGANISE A MAJOR TOUR

Jealousy: that's what started the Giro d'Italia. A little jealousy, a lot of revenge and a long simmering row. Almost a vendetta. All rather Italian, in fact.

These days the Giro is the world's second biggest stage race, smaller only than the Tour de France. You'd think it would have had glorious beginnings, gestured and kissed into shape in the land of style and grandeur. But instead of that it began in the grubbiest way: because a spiteful sales rep fell out with Bianchi and was looking for revenge.

The daily sports paper behind the Giro even in those days was the *Gazzetta dello Sport*. Now it's part of a huge publishing group, printed by the million in time to be read with morning coffee in the Mediterranean sun. But the paper was so short of money in its earliest days, in 1908, that the typesetters and journalists left each night not at all sure there'd be any pay for them at the end of the week. The last thing the paper could afford was a Giro d'Italia. Even the staff of *Gazzetta dello Sport* was astonished. Especially the directors who took the decision.

Among the most surprised was Armando Cougnet, just 18 years old and a man of 6 feet 2 inches who was paid 120 lire a month to edit the paper's cycling pages. He was on a business trip to Venice, promoting his paper's sales because, not yet 70 issues old, it didn't look as though it would survive without all the promotion it could get. And then he received a telegram: ABSOLUTELY ESSENTIAL FOR THE PAPER YOU ANNOUNCE IMMEDIATELY THE CYCLING TOUR OF ITALY.

"What? Essential? 'Absolutely essential'? A race like the Tour de France? For *this* struggling little paper? Me? Oh, come on..."

The same news had gone by telegram to Camillo Costamagna at his home in Mondovì. Costamagna may have been the newspaper's main director but his pay was only 30 lire a month more than that of his youthful cycling editor. He too ran his eyes down to the signature … Tullo Morgagni, the man he had employed as editor and the shortest of the three in height.

It wasn't easy to make a phone call in 1908 and travel was also difficult. So not until Cougnet had returned home and Costamagna had travelled to the *Gazzetta*'s offices at 2 via della Signora on August 6, the next day, did the two men find out what had happened. They went straight to Morgagni's office, where he gestured them to seats in a corner and started to explain.

"I've heard from Angelo Gatti," he said. The others didn't need to be told that Gatti had worked for Bianchi, Italy's most prestigious bike company, that he had a row there and left as a bitter enemy. Now he ran the rival Atala factory. Morgagni explained that Gatti had been to the Bologna bike show and, happy to hear anything he could use to annoy his former employer, had learned from an acquaintance called Tomaselli that Bianchi was involved in a new Giro d'Italia. It was to be a three-part venture, Bianchi supplying the biking expertise, the Touring Club Italiano lending the experience of its round-Italy car rally, and the *Corriere della Sera* putting up the cash and the publicity.

The *Corriere* was the *Gazzetta*'s bigger and more established rival. Just as Gatti wanted to damage Bianchi, so the *Gazzetta* had to knock *Corriere*, merely to survive.

"I just thought you'd be interested to know," Gatti had said with a smirk, knowing that passing on an industrial secret was a damaging stab at Bianchi. Now they were all involved in the plot, Gatti because he could continue his vendetta against Bianchi, the newsmen because they had inside information about their giant rival and had to act quickly. They had to decide and it didn't take them long. Decisions never do when they're driven by emotion.

The three journalists sat at a solid, black and upright typewriter and concocted an announcement. On August 7, 1908, in paper number 71, it appeared on the front page: the *Gazzetta dello Sport* was going to organise a Giro d'Italia the following May.

Cougnet recalled: "It was pretty easy to announce a Giro but the realities soon hit us, because we were broke." The cost turned out to be 25,000 lire, which means nothing now after so many years of inflation and didn't matter then, either, because however much it was, they didn't have it. They didn't even have the money for the first prize, which they set at 3,000 lire for no reason, it seems, than that it sounded a good round figure. It was also more than half again what Costamagna was paid for a whole year, but what the heck? If you're going to go bankrupt whether you organise a Giro d'Italia or not, why not go ahead and run it?

It was then that the three remembered a mutual friend called Bongrani, who worked for a local bank. There was no way a bank was going to lend them money and Bongrani said so, but he added that the way banks grew rich was by collecting small sums from a lot of people. Put them together and they came to a fortune. That, he said, was what he'd do for the Giro. He took time off from the bank and literally went knocking on doors to ask for money.

Then something even more Biblical happened. Far from resenting the newcomer's snatching their idea, the people at *Corriere* were impressed by the enthusiasm and began to see that if the *Gazzetta* had keenness if not cash, and if the race was going to go ahead anyway, it could itself put up the 3,000 lire first prize. That way it kept in the running whatever happened, and for a lot less effort and money than it had expected, and it forced Costamagna and his crew to publicise their own paper, the *Corriere*.

That in turn inspired the Italian cycling association, which had been jealous of the developing Tour de France on the other side of the mountains, and it put in a further 13,900 lire. That left Bongrani and the others to come up with only 8,000. They abandoned the backstreet door-knocking and begged it from the Sghirla engineering company, the casino at San Remo, and other concerns. The world's second biggest stage race was on. The future of its organising paper was rather less certain and it could still have gone under at any moment. The directors at *Corriere* probably even hoped that it would. Letting their impertinent little rival have the Giro d'Italia would probably force it out of business, they reckoned. If that happened, they would get its circulation, its advertising *and* its race for just the 3,000 lire it had provided.

On May 13, 1909, the organisers spent the morning signing on 127 of the 166 riders who'd entered. They were in the Piazza Loreto in Milan. Ten years later Benito Mussolini would start the Fascist movement and 36 years later, in that same square, he and his mistress, Clara Petacci, would be hanged upside down after being shot by partisans by Lake Como as they fled for the Swiss border.

Unencumbered for the moment by the swinging body of a portly dictator, the race set off at 2:53 PM for the first of the 2,448 km that would take it to Bologna, Chieti, Naples, Rome, Florence, Genoa, Turin and Milan in eight stages. Only 49 riders made it. News of their progress was posted in the windows of the Peugeot bike shop in the Piazza Loreto and those richer Italians who had telephones could call the shop on Milan 3368 and have the details read to them.

Public reaction was enormous. Crowds lined the stage into Milan and soldiers were hired to escort the four dozen who made it all the way. *Gazzetta dello Sport*, admittedly not an impartial observer, reported: "Standards flying in the wind on their galloping mounts, the lancers joined the first finishers for the last kilometers. After Dario Beni's [stage] victory, vehicles of the fire brigade carried the competitors to The Arena, where the crowd carried Ganna in triumph. A glorious event has been deeply inscribed in the annals of sport, to be repeated yearly with growing enthusiasm and love."

Ganna was Luigi Ganna. He was head of the Atala team, Atala being the company of Angelo Gatti whose vendetta with Bianchi had got the whole thing started. He won 5,325 lire, a fortune then, and certainly enough to ruin the organising newspaper had the race not succeeded. The irony is that by the time Italy switched to the euro, 5,325 lire was probably just about enough to buy a single copy of *Gazzetta dello Sport* and a coffee to drink with it.

Gazzetta dello Sport ran the Giro up to 1988, when the race moved to RCS Organizzazioni Sportivi, in the same building as *Gazzetta* but separate from it. It also runs the Tour of Lombardy, Milan–San Remo, Milan–Turin and others. *Corriere della Sera* prospered as well. It and the *Gazzetta dello Sport* are now such good friends that they're part of the same company.

34

HOW NOT TO ORGANISE A MAJOR TOUR

I expect you think that the Tour de France goes only to carefully chosen places. Never, you'd think, could be any idea of a man scratching his head in Paris and being grateful for suggestions. It is here that I shall tell you of my own part in creating international cycling history, how I diverted the Tour de France. I was proud of it at the time. Since then it's been something I've kept quiet about …

The first job I had as a journalist was on the staff of *Cycling*, a weekly magazine published then in the center of the London newspaper business, in Fleet Street. The newspapers have moved on since then but they, and *Cycling*, are still going. I left in about 1972 because I couldn't stand it any more but I must still have been happy to take the magazine's money because I immediately wrote an article imagining what it would be like if the Tour came to Britain.

The editor had dismissed it as a ridiculous thought when I actually worked there but he must have been taken by my fanciful description of colourful jerseys and sparkling wheels heading up the main road from Dover to London because he published it. I pocketed the cheque and thought no more of it. It had never occurred to me that the Tour, like everywhere else, has men with blank days, days when the ideas just don't come. Never had it occurred to me that *L'Équipe*, which in those days was much closer to the Tour, would run a story headlined BRITANNIQUES WANT THE TOUR. Someone there had read my article and taken it as a semi-official invitation.

The rest of my dream also took shape without my knowing it. Somebody read that *L'Équipe* article in an office on the Brittany coast and took it in to show his boss, a busy and far-sighted man called Alexis

Gourvennec. Rural France knew him well, and the government in Paris, too, because his campaign for a better deal for farmers had made Brittany almost a no-go area for ministers and civil servants alike.

Gourvennec's latest battle had been to save the region's artichoke farmers from having to drive their crop all the way to the north-west coast at Calais to export it to Britain. The first trading borders had just fallen in Europe and Gourvennec saw Britain as an unexploited area for sales but, equally, he saw the day-long truck journey to Calais as an obstacle. When the established ferry companies told him there was no suitable port nearer Brittany, Gourvennec's solution was to talk the government into paying for one at Roscoff. And when nobody would run ships there, he and his fellow farmers got together to run their own, from Roscoff to Plymouth, in south-west England. It started in 1973 and the company still operates to this day, known as Brittany Ferries.

Anyway, one thing leads to another and Gourvennec now needed to promote not only artichokes but his ferry. And that's where the little newspaper story brought to him that day came to his help. The Tour, he suggested or more probably demanded, would go to England on his ferry. The following year. The Tour would race in Plymouth and he would take with it a very large supply of artichokes to hand out to puzzled Englishman whose exotic food, as all Frenchmen know, was limited to sausages and milky tea.

Cycling, the magazine which had mocked my idea when I worked there, threw itself into events with Biblical zeal. This would be the nation's event of a lifetime; unbelieving infidels would abandon soccer in favour of a *real* sport and the very air would be sweeter to breathe.

Until that point I was enormously proud. I had doubts about Plymouth, which is a long way from anywhere else in England, and my heart didn't sing when I read that the stage would be held up and down an unopened bypass, round a roundabout at one end and back round another one in the other. It wasn't the legendary ride to London that I'd imagined. But, heck, I was the man who'd made it happen and I wasn't responsible for the details. One day people would thank me and talk of my vision and drive.

I and two friends went to Plymouth, where local cyclists had laid on a week of racing to support the Tour. There weren't, I admit, as many people there as I'd expected but I was sure they'd turn up nearer the day. They did, but nowhere near as many as the faithful—and *Cycling*—believed. I stayed on a camp site and there was still plenty of space.

Unknown to me and to everyone else in Plymouth, things had started going wrong. On the other side of the Channel, the advertising caravan had decided to stay in France. The people who fling out cheap junk from the back of trucks dressed up as dead flies or vacuum cleaners weren't going to pay for a long crossing to a country where nobody knew the products they were selling and where the race just went up and down a bypass. It was miserable as it was, driving a huge dead plastic fly round France to advertise insect spray; to go to some awful wet country where everyone knew the food was dreadful and where the fly spray wasn't on sale anyway was out of the question. Much better to spend a couple of days behind a Pernod outside a French bar and wait for Le Tour to return to civilisation.

The riders didn't want to go either, but they had no choice. "It was ridiculous," Michel Pollentier told me years afterwards, "going all that way just to ride a criterium." At least the riders arrived by plane. Their bikes came on the ship and British Customs officers, never having seen so many at one time and not accepting that riders would need more than one apiece, impounded the lot and discussed charging import tax.

There was worse for Jacques Goddet, the man whom Gourvennec had persuaded to take the race and his artichokes across the water in the first place. He'd never needed to take his passport before when the race had left France with the Tour. He didn't think he'd need it this time. But he did. It took him a long time to get through British immigration controls, pleading his case in excellent English (Goddet went to school in England) but with an intransigent border clerk who knew nothing of the Tour de France, nothing of Jacques Goddet, but a lot about people who tried to get into other people's countries without the right papers.

All this made for a potent mixture. Unaware of any of it, we fans turned up at the roadside to watch. We noticed there were fewer of us than we'd expected but that, we were sure, was because the main crowds were somewhere else round the course. I was still prepared to tell anybody who'd listen that it had all been my idea. After the first hour I was less keen. After the second hour I had learned to keep quiet.

The riders, resentful at once more being messed around by the Tour de France and its wish to go to abnormal places in return for money, made the stage as boring as its course. They rode up and down all day in a sullen bunch, not even making a token effort at providing a spirited last hour. They started in a bunch and finished in a bunch, fairly fast, but very much cycling's equivalent of a slow, nil-nil draw on a muddy pitch at a half-full soccer stadium.

Next day, one of the country's biggest newspapers, the *Daily Mirror*, ran an enormous headline across its sports pages. It said: TOUR DE FRANCE: CAN 40 MILLION FRENCHMEN BE WRONG?

35

HOW TO SURVIVE THE COLD

Some races are hard because the course is hard. Others are made hard by the weather. In 1956, for instance, a howling gale carried snow to the Merano–Bondone stage of the Giro d'Italia, even though it was June. Riders abandoned by the dozen. By the end of the day there were 57 fewer riders left in the race. Crossing the Dolomites was always going to be hard but this was something different.

The little Luxembourg rider Charly Gaul, though, rode on almost oblivious to the temperature. Well, if not oblivious then certainly comforted, because his team manager, Learco Guerra, had the brilliant idea of stopping to fill two huge wash tubs with hot water so his rider could thaw his frozen limbs. Gaul soared on in the snow on the Monte Bondone until he'd made up the 15 minutes that the stars had had on him and then gained enough to win the Giro as well. He won three stages that year and launched his reputation as the man who triumphed in bad weather but, equally true, suffered in the heat.

Suffering even more was Fiorenzo Magni who, not only cold, was riding with a broken shoulder and pulling on the bars with the help of a length of inner tube gripped in his teeth. Despite that he came second.

The cold hit Bernard Hinault as well, but even so he won Liège–Bastogne–Liège by 10 minutes in 1980. Once more a polar wind whipped the riders from the start and the snow began as soon as the race had climbed out of Liège. The flakes turned into a blizzard and riders struggled on with hands pressed across their eyes to keep a view of the road. The normally colourful doyen of classics was transformed into a mass of anonymous plastic jackets and windcheaters. Spectators stood in goggles, like red-faced snowmen. Riders pulled out two dozen at a time, men like Gibi Baronchelli and Beppe Saronni, and

Lucien van Impe and Jean-René Bernaudeau. Some teams had barely a man left on the road after the first hour.

Hinault passed Maurice Le Guilloux, his only team-mate left riding. He told him he was pulling out. Le Guilloux shouted: "Carry on to Bastogne. There's a feeding station there. Pack it in then if you want to but don't do it now." Both dropped back through the dwindling bunch to find their manager, Cyrille Guimard, and some dry gloves. Another dozen riders called it a day, the drop-out rate averaging a man a minute for the first hour.

"At this rate we won't have a race at all," someone said on the race radio. There was a pause and a muffled discussion. And then: "Attention team managers: the commissaires have agreed that warm drinks can be passed to riders at any stage of the race."

The snow had turned to rain by the time Hinault reached Bastogne. Only 21 riders began the journey back to Liège. The last, Jostein Wilmann, was 27 minutes down. Hinault said: "Cyrille Guimard told me to remove my racing cape because the real race was about to start. My cape was made of waxed fabric and I was very warm inside it, but I took it off as instructed. Until then I hadn't really paid any attention to the race, but now my teeth were chattering and I had no protection. I decided the only thing to do was ride as hard as I could to keep myself warm."

Rudy Pévenage and Ludo Peeters had broken away before the Côte de Wanna, which is 2.8 km at 4.9 percent and the shallowest of the principal climbs. Hinault was on a fresh bike, having swapped at the feed at Wielsam, and went off up the slope. The Côte de Stockeu that followed was the same length but 9.6 percent. Hinault made up time, and then, on the Haute-Levée he caught and dropped them.

"The rhythm had returned and I was feeling good," he said. "I didn't even need to turn round to know that my pursuers had vanished."

He rode into the boulevard de la Sauvinière in Liège to the cheers of his team and of the pitiful crowd but with no feeling in his arms. It took three weeks to get proper movement back into the index and middle fingers of his right hand and even now they ache in cold weather. A bath waited at the hotel but he couldn't get in until the water was almost cold; the contrast was too great.

It snowed next year as well and only a couple of dozen finished. The winner, Johan van der Velde, was disqualified and the decision went to Josef Fuchs of Switzerland. Those with long memories recalled the same race in 1957. The race could barely pass any of Belgium's many roadside bars without yet another rider disappearing inside to press himself into the drinkers for warmth. That was the year when the giant Frenchman, Gérard Saint, stopped in the snow to piss on his hands to bring them back to life.

Germain Derycke reached the finish alone that year, his skin raw with coldness. And then, as if there hadn't been misery enough, the judges disqualified him for jumping over a closed railroad crossing. They gave the victory to the runner-up, Frans Schoubben, although the Belgian federation overruled them and made the two joint winners.

That year, the world champion Louison Bobet finished way down the field. When, like Hinault, he got to his hotel and found his team washed, warm and dry, his team-manager ordered: "Gentlemen, rise! A great champion is entering the room."

And just to make you realise that you really ought to go out on your bike and not kid yourself it's cold out there, remember the Tour in 1948. That had weather so bad that only 44 of the 120 starters finished. The French writer Pierre Chany said he came across Apo Lazarides "standing frozen on the quagmire descent of the Galibier, a candle of ice hanging from his chin." And then, in a phrase that just strikes cold into the spine, that just up the road he had passed two Italians sharing a single pair of leg-warmers.

36

HOW TO SURVIVE THE HEAT (1)

The French word *canicule* means oppressive, stifling heat when the air is thick and refuses to move and dogs can't raise the energy to scratch themselves. The was just such a day in the Tour de France of 1935, when the riders faced a long hot 17th day from Bordeaux to Pau. The speed was as low—just 13 mph—as their spirits. Men just rode without talking, their legs as dead and listless as their minds.

And then, like men in a desert, they saw an unbelievable sight: ahead of them, waving to them temptingly, were rows of spectators behind tables laden with cool beer. In adventure films the mirage disappears and the oasis turns out to be no more than more burning, featureless sand. But this time the cold drink didn't shimmer into thin air. It stayed on the tables. Or rather, it passed into the spectators' offering hands and from them to the reaching hands of the grateful riders. The slow-bicycle race of the Tour de France had come to a complete and unscheduled halt as riders downed drinks and some loaded the pockets of their thick woolen jerseys with more.

Only one rider decided he wasn't thirsty enough to stop. His name was Julien Moineau, which means "sparrow" in French. The bunch had forgotten about him in the clammy heat and the misery of their jobs but if anyone had cared to remember he would have recalled that Moineau had been the centre of both interest and ridicule at the start of the day. He had turned up with a 52-tooth chainring, common these days but unheard of then. Seeing the other riders stop for beer, he pulled on his gear lever, shifted his chain on to this monstrosity, turned it as hard as he could and won the stage by 15:33. He even stood by the finish line to toast the bunch with a beer as it followed him in.

As well he might. He had organised the stunt himself. The generous beer people with their roadside table were all his friends and he'd asked other friends in the bunch to help delay the race as much as possible. He wasn't a total no-hoper because he came second in Bordeaux–Paris in May 1935 and third the previous year and fourth the year before that. But his beer-stained win in the Tour de France was the highlight of his career. He died in 1980 when he was 69.

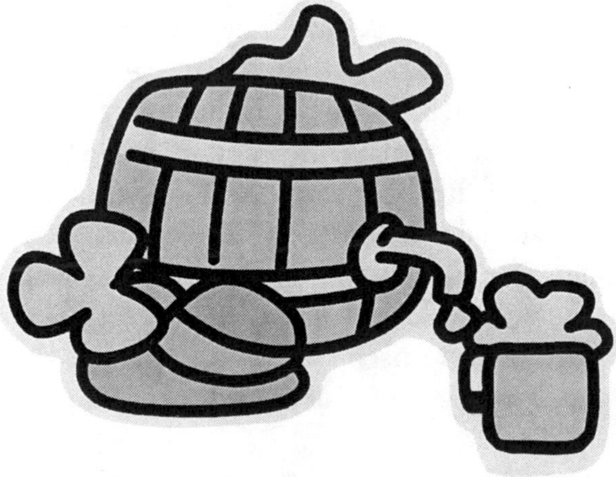

37

HOW TO SURVIVE THE HEAT (2)

In 1950 the little fishing town of St-Tropez hadn't yet gained the reputation it has now. The smart set, sun-seekers and Parisian artists hadn't arrived. Brigitte Bardot hadn't yet met Roger Vadim and not until 1956 would she flounce in a bikini in *And God Created Woman*. In fact bikinis had been presented to a sometimes outraged world only four years earlier and Louis Réard, the designer, had had to hire a stripper to model one because established models were too prudish.

The village of Ste-Maxime across the bay was still less known. Just 2,600 people lived there instead of the 12,000 today and most were still only just coming to terms with the tourists and artists who'd started to discover them thanks to improvements to the Cogolin–Fréjus highway. But on July 28, 1950, Ste-Maxime was to be projected into the forefront of world publicity in a way it could never have expected.

The Tour de France was on its 14th stage, running along the Mediterranean coast from the naval city of Toulon to the town of Menton. That day too was a *canicule* and the only action other than sullen pedalling came as riders passed streams or fountains and gratefully filled their bottles or rinsed their faces. Now and then obliging spectators showered the riders with garden hoses and the race would go even more slowly to make the most of the cold water.

Then the road turned suddenly down to the bay at Ste-Maxime. For the first time all day the race came to action. Apo "the Greek kid" Lazarides shouted: "I'm going in, *les gars!*", and he rode his bike straight down to the beach. In a handful of seconds more than 60 others had followed him, some not getting off their bikes but riding straight over the shingle and then the band of sand before plunging into the cool water of the Mediterranean.

Jacques Goddet, the race organiser, stood furious but powerless at the roadside. Powerless for the instant, anyway. Later that day the 62 impromptu sea-bathers had another chilling experience. That evening's race bulletin listed penalties for all of them.

38

HOW TO SURVIVE THE HEAT (3)

Apo Lazarides, who thanks to his nine toes will return to our story later, wasn't the only one to feel the heat that day. In fact the only people who weren't troubled were a novel North African team, made up of riders born in France's colonies or overseas departments along the continent's coast.

There was no great experience in the team, either in the riders or in the manager, who was a journalist called Tony Arbano, who worked for *Dépêche Quotidienne* in Algiers and wrote sports stories in his spare time for *L'Équipe*. Among the riders was Abdel-Khader Zaaf from Chibli in Algeria, a country at that time not yet independent from France.

It is not unknown for riders to go the wrong way in the Tour de France. The French writer Antoine Blondin said of Mont Ventoux: "There are few happy memories of this sorcerer's cauldron. We have seen riders reduced to madness under the effect of the heat or stimulants, some coming back down the hairpins they thought they were climbing, others brandishing their pumps and accusing us of murder." Few riders, however, have gone the wrong way either as publicly or as convincingly as Abdel-Khader Zaaf.

His troubles started when he decided to attack, with his team-mate Marcel Molines, on a stinking hot stage from Perpignan to Nîmes. It was July 28, the same summer—1950—as the impromptu dip in the sea at Ste-Maxime. That day, too, nobody wanted to race. Zaaf and Molines therefore had no resistance when they set off with 200 km to go, even when they got enough lead to make Zaaf the Tour's leader on the road. Had the two stayed clear he would have become the Tour's first African yellow jersey. Either he or Molines would have been the first black rider to win a stage, a record that in the end went to Molines because he stayed away.

The reason that Zaaf didn't become the first non-white *maillot jaune* was that he began zig-zagging with 15 km to go. He went slower and slower and took such ever-increasing slices of the road that in the end an official could stand it no more and tugged him off his bike. Zaaf protested that he wanted to continue and began to gesticulate and shout as the official attempted to prevent him. But he wobbled more when he set off once again and that was enough for him and for everyone else. He was led into the shade and propped up against a tree to wait for the race ambulance. Before long he fell asleep.

The bunch, though, was in no hurry and communications weren't what they are now. Both meant that it took a long time for the medical men to arrive. Before they had, Zaaf had regained consciousness, stared in panic at the crowd that had gathered around him, and then jumped up in alarm and got back on his bike. Unfortunately he then set off in the wrong direction, his eyes glassy, his head confused, his legs buckling. Spectators pulled him off again and kept him off his bike until the ambulance arrived. He was then taken away under doctors' orders.

The legend has grown that Zaaf was overcome by the heat and perhaps by dehydration, because in those days riders believed they should drink as little as they could. They followed the rule expressed later by Jacques Anquetil as "driest is fastest." The legend goes on to say that Zaaf was drunk when he set off in the wrong direction, that a spectator had tried to revive him with a bottle of wine. That, it's said, went to Zaaf's head quicker than usual because as a Muslim he had never previously drunk alcohol.

Well, it's a nice story, but possibly less than the truth. How much wine could you force through the lips of a man too groggy to ride his bike? How much wine would a devout Muslim drink before he realised what it was and refused it in horror? And, given that few people like alcohol at their first taste, how much would he have managed before recoiling? And anyway, how much would you need to drink to become so dizzy that you'd ride off the wrong way in something as important to you as the Tour de France?

Further doubt comes from his recollection that "After the Tour everyone wanted to drink a glass of wine with me. I couldn't refuse but

I drank far too much." Zaaf had either speedily renounced Islam or he was talking of lemonade while others drank wine. Less charitable reports talk of drugs, the obsession and confusion of amphetamine (which hot days made dangerously effective) coupled with dehydration.

Whatever the reason, Zaaf asked to ride the missing distance, like Hippolyte Pagie years before, before the next day's stage. That way he would be last on the stage and even last in the race but he would still be in the Tour. The organisers had had enough, though. They didn't want precedents like that in modern times, they didn't want dubious cases, and they didn't want to be messed about and embarrassed by riders who should know how to behave themselves. Zaaf was out.

The incident both made and destroyed him. Initially it made him a celebrity and he could raise his fee in the criteriums that followed the Tour from $50 to $500, the kind of money that only the best stars could demand. And then, still while he was a name on every spectator's lips, he vanished. He became just another legend of the Tour, the kind of man whose name is preceded by the words "I wonder whatever happened to ..."

And that's how it stayed until January 27, 1982, and a cold day at a train station in Paris. A passenger on the platform stepped aside to make way for a shuffling old man coming the other way. He smiled at the old chap in response to his mumbled thanks, then stared at his back as he moved slowly away. A moment later he caught him up again and a moment after that he said: "Excuse me, *monsieur*, but do I perhaps recognise you?"

And then out came the story. Zaaf had had a gap in his run of engagements and gone back to his home in Algeria. That night a soldier investigating smugglers and other tax evaders had knocked at his door, demanding to see his papers. The soldier looked at them and demanded Zaaf go to the police station with him. Zaaf explained that he had only just returned from racing in France and that he was too tired to go. Could he not go the next day? He moved his hand to the lock of the door and the policeman interpreted it as an attempt to reach for a gun and shot him in the leg as he began to close the door.

The wound wasn't serious—policemen's guns fire only small bullets, although they leave a mess at short range—and Zaaf was left unseen in the hospital until the morning. Then his injuries were patched and he was thrown into the rough Baroughia jail as a smuggling suspect. And the police may well have found the right man. Zaaf went two years without trial and lost all he owned except, as he admitted himself, some hidden money. Honest money is usually banked, not hidden.

Zaaf said he had developed diabetes in the hospital, and that had damaged his sight and he had come to Paris for an operation. The news got out quickly after that, of course. A lot had happened between 1950 and 1982. For a start, Algerians had fought a long and bloody war of independence which had ended only in 1962. More than 15,000 French soldiers and an untold number of Algerians had died. Stories emerged, at first denied and then confirmed, that French soldiers had regularly tortured Algerians to extract information from them. Much of France was at best confused about what had happened and frequently embarrassed. Zaaf's reappearance coincided with the 20th anniversary of the end of the war and it provided a focus for those feelings. Fans sent telegrams, flowers and presents.

Zaaf had his operation and his eyes improved. He was only 53 that day he shuffled along the platform but his life was already coming to an end. He returned to Algeria and died four years later, for ever remembered as The Man Who Went the Wrong Way.

And Marcel Molines, the man who actually won the stage? He died on September 22, 1986, with not a single other notable success to his name.

39

HOW TO SURVIVE THE HEAT (4)

The first African I've found to have ridden the Tour, and I don't claim it as a proven record, was an 18-year-old Tunisian called Ali Neffati. He rode in 1913 after getting his first bike only a night or two earlier. He rode the Tour because, well, in those days he could. It was open to anyone.

Anyway, despite his inexperience, Neffati rode well, always wearing a fez. Reporters loved him, of course, because if there was nothing else to report they could always spend a few words on this exotic novelty in regional dress. And so it was that they wrote that on one of the hottest days, a 470 km stage from Brest to La Rochelle, Henri Desgrange drove up alongside and asked him: "You're not too hot, *mon petit*?" To which Neffati said "No, no *missié* [African dialect for *monsieur*] Desgrange, I'm actually rather too cold."

Perhaps he wasn't telling the whole truth. Whatever the reason, he climbed off and neither finished the Tour nor started another. Desgrange never forgot him, though, and gave him a job as a messenger at his paper, *L'Auto*, and he moved to *L'Équipe* after the war.

Since Nefatti and the brief appearance decades later of the team from North Africa, the Tour de France has remained a persistently white race for the white race despite the UCI's wish to make cycling more of a world sport.

40

HOW TO SAVE THE DAY

Somewhere in France is a man called Michaël. You can tell he's young because for decades people in France were allowed to name their children only after saints and the saint in France is Michel and not the more Germanic or English Michaël.

Michaël was too young to drive a car or even a full-scale motorbike. Instead he had a moped, a little noisy machine with embryo-like pedals to give it the status of just a powered bicycle. And on that he has acquired saint-like, or at any rate legendary, status. Possibly France's only saint on a moped but not to be mocked simply for that …

Michaël was 16 in 1990 and lived near the village of St-Gemme. He may still be there. There were two things he knew that summer, the first that the Tour de France was coming through the village and the second that a bunch of his neighbours, all of them angry sheep farmers, may have been planning to make sure it didn't.

The Union Paysanne, the farmers' union, was upset at imports of mutton from eastern Europe which they said threatened their livelihood. At the same time, they protested, the European quota system was limiting their own production. They could have only a limited number of animals as Europe sought to come to terms with years of agricultural over-production. The EU's Common Agricultural Policy is still a bitter subject for many French farmers.

That day's stage of the Tour started in Poitiers and planned to reach Nantes after 233 km. Steve Bauer was a surprise *maillot jaune* for Canada and the American 7-Eleven team and this otherwise unremarkable stage was expected to be only a personal battle between Bauer and another English-speaker, the Irishman Stephen Roche.

What made it clear from the start that it was perhaps not to be as much of a ho-hum day as many thought was the arrival of farmers at the start at Poitiers. There they presented a live lamb decked out in ribbons not to the winners of the previous day's team time-trial but to the Spanish Kelme team, which had come last. The organisers looked on tolerantly as Fabio Parra accepted it on behalf of the team and then displayed it for the cameras. The moment gave Kelme more publicity than had anything the previous day.

In the officials' mind, though, was the memory of the first day. Then, as Claudio Chiappucci gathered enough points on the small hills around Futuroscope to build his stake for the King of the Mountains title, straw bales, diesel oil and branches of trees had appeared on the road at La Puye after the lead cars had passed but ahead of the riders. Chiappucci and his group swerved around them without too much trouble but the main race had been delayed.

The Union Paysanne denied responsibility for that and so the presentation of a lamb to Fabio Parra, while laden with irony, could possibly be regarded as a sign of solidarity with the Tour, possibly even an apology. But farmers are powerful people in France and they're known for their direct action. This, after all, is a nation founded on revolution and action in the streets. Jean-Marie Leblanc and the other organisers noted what had happened and stood prepared for worse.

They didn't have to wait long. St-Gemme came 85 km after the start, not in sheep country so much as among cattle pasture. All the same, the farmers' discontent was widespread enough for Leblanc to take the hint that the village was close to France's biggest abattoir at Bressure, that there were four trees felled and lined up by the roadside, and that agricultural types were playing pétanque beside them. Conveniently, they also had a tractor capable of shifting the fallen trees. Reports from scouts sent out ahead of the race also reported smoke drifting across the road from burning tires. Banners were being erected to accuse the president, François Mitterand, of ruining the rural economy.

Just up the road was kilometer 92 of the stage, significant only because French *départements* are numbered according to their position in the alphabet. St-Gemme is in *département* 92 and it had laid on a press reception at kilometer 92. There would be no shortage of reporters to report the farmers' discontent if anything happened.

Only the blind or blindly optimistic could have taken another decision: Jean-Marie Leblanc stopped the race 10 km before the village. Riders got off, few of them knowing what had happened and many of them just happy to have a rest. Officials got out of their cars and those who didn't take the moment to stretch their legs or pee by the roadside got out maps and spread them across the bonnets of their cars to work out a detour. It wasn't going to be easy; they were on a direct road with no obvious diversion.

And then, with a brittle putt-putt of his single exhaust pipe, along came heavenly intervention seated on a moped. St Michaël had arrived. St Michaël explained that he knew the area as only a local could know it. Perhaps he could be of service. Could he invite the Tour de France to follow him through the little-known lanes which would take it behind the waiting protesters?

Legend insists that the greatest sporting event in the world fell gratefully in line behind its youthful saviour and for 25 km followed obediently at the best speed that a 50cc vélomoteur could manage before he got it back on the main road again. As the British reporter Geoffrey Nicholson pointed out: "It seems unlikely that the race *direction* and the gendarmerie … couldn't have found their own way but the press know a good legend in the making when they see one."

Michaël will probably still accept the offer of a beer to tell his story, should you ever find yourself in his village. If you go there on September 29, so much the better. That's St Michel's day in France—the closest he'll get to being a real saint.

41

HOW TO FOLLOW ORDERS

Somewhere in a bar in Marseille there was a Tour de France rider's toe, preserved in formaldehyde and kept in a bottle. Two brothers owned it. I say "owned", in the past tense, because of course it may no longer be there. But it's not every day you have a chance to see a bottle with a Tour rider's toe in it, so you may want to try finding it next time you're there.

By now, of course, you're wondering how such a thing could be. And you'd like the answer. Well, you shall not be disappointed …

The man it belonged to was René Vietto, whom legend inaccurately says rose from being a hotel lift attendant in Cannes to one of the best riders who never quite won the Tour de France. In 1934 he gave up very real chances to win in order to help Antonin Magne, his team leader; in 1935 he won a stage but was held up by the year's crashes; in 1936 he had a painful knee and he was demoralised because a charlatan had mis-invested his money; in 1937 and 1938 he didn't ride; and in 1939 his knee gave way in the mountains.

The Tour returned from the war in 1947 and Vietto, now 33 and with three knee operations behind him, won the yellow jersey by riding alone for 130 km between Lille and Brussels. He lost it after a week, then regained it in the Alps, and then he lost it in a time-trial three days from the end. Once more the greatest prize had escaped him.

Vietto was a poor time-triallist but a great climber obsessed by weight. He'd pare bits off his bike here, experiment with improbably light equipment there. And in 1947 he had a toe cut off. It was troubling him anyway, so he told the doctor: "Take this toe off. It's gone bad." Off it came a few days later and Vietto laughed: "Like that, I'll be lighter in the mountains." It then somehow ended up in a bottle of formaldehyde in Marseille and I've always been determined to find it.

What makes the story really strange is that having lost his own toe, Vietto turned to his best domestique, Apo Lazarides, and ordered him to lose a toe as well.

"But why?" Lazarides protested, not wholly unreasonably. "I don't need to."

"Because I say so," said Vietto, and such was his command over the man's life that Lazarides went ahead. For the rest of his life he walked with a wobble.

Poor Lazarides' misery didn't end even when Vietto stopped racing and took over the management of the Helyett team, sponsored by a French bike factory. Good bosses will usually pound the desk with employees in private but defend them in public. But not Vietto. He never wasted a moment on diplomacy and it seemed never to occur to him that his riders would go better if he spoke up for them a bit more. After the 1951 Giro, for instance, he said: "I have never attended such a long funeral; it was 5,000 km long and my team followed the whole way. They call themselves racers but they were more like mourners."

Lazarides had joined Vietto's Helyett team but he soon found his hope should have been overruled by experience. He got nothing but criticism. Whatever went wrong, it was because he hadn't tried hard enough. He even got it in the neck when Vietto took some of the team to the opera at La Scala. The riders were sitting as hushed as everyone else as a lone singer stunned them with her performance. And then in the middle of her performance, Vietto hissed: "Apo?"

It wasn't at all the thing to do and the audience went "Sssh!" But Vietto persisted…

"Apo…" he said again.

"Yes, René?"

"Apo, you see the woman on the stage?"

Lazarides said he did.

"What about her?" he asked.

"Well she at least is doing what she's paid for, you bastard."

There was at least sometimes a little happiness in the poor man's life: he came second to Briek Schotte in the 1948 world championship, just one second from the rainbow jersey. To be truly happy, of course, he'd have won.

He stopped racing in 1956 and died in Nice in 1998 after a long illness, aged 73 and with nine toes. He is still mourned by the Left. His pre-war peak coincided with important social changes in France, not least the first paid vacations. Getting wages to stand beside the road to cheer on *coureurs* was a novelty that few resisted and picnics on the verge were never so numerous.

The change came because France despaired of leaders who favored business and the church and elected a left-wing government instead. The socialists were the majority and not the communists, whose supporters nevertheless saw it as a call to revolution and took to the streets until their leaders told them to go back home again.

Vietto was a communist and spoke about it openly. The communist newspaper, *L'Humanité*, constantly reminded roadside crowds that it was the Left that had won them their time off and referred to the excellent riding of "Comrade Vietto."

Nothing could be better than that Comrade Vietto had to give up his chances for those of Antonin Magne. Perfect illustration of management exploitation, *n'est-ce pas?*

Aux armes, citoyens! *

*"To arms, citizens!", from the chorus of the *Marseillaise*.

42

HOW TO BE JUST A LITTLE TOO GOOD (1)

Not even the most passionate cycling fan would claim that all criteriums aren't tinged with just a little show and entertainment. These round-the-houses races were for years ridden only by local riders. In an era when travel was more difficult, the big riders stayed at home when there was no race worth the effort of going to. And criteriums, in out-of-the-way villages, weren't worth going to.

Then in the 1950s along came agents such as Daniel Dousset and Roger Piel in France and Jean van Buggenhout in Belgium. They set up stables of riders and, in van Buggenhout's case, administered races and teams. Each in his way became a puppet-master, controlling riders' lives through their race contracts, their team contracts and their appearance money.

The writer William Fotheringham said: "It was a cartel. If a cyclist was not on one of the agents' books he had no appearance money: nothing to live off other than prize money and whatever his team might pay him. As a result, the agent-rider relationship was one of dependence on the riders' side, exploitation on that of the manager … Dousset or Piel could always find new riders; the riders had nowhere else to turn. It was effectively a form of tied labour."

The agents profited particularly from the change in village races from local derbies to a chance to attract *les Tourmen*. Every rider who finished the Tour had his price, from first to last, and with team retainers for most being low or even non-existent—even the biggest teams rarely paid all its riders, the rest racing for just a share of the prizes and simply for the lifestyle—criteriums were where most riders made the bulk of their money.

From the 1950s until the 1970s they could ride almost daily, sometimes twice a day. The system ended only when wages rose sharply in the Greg LeMond period, after which riders no longer needed to ride criteriums and began asking a lot more to persuade them that they should. Those events that survived the increased financial demands range from the genuine if deliberately colourful to those that are simply rigged so the public gets to see whom it paid to see.

The French rider Erwann Menthéour wrote in his book of confessions, *Secret Défonce* [*Secret High*, being on a drug high]: "The script of a criterium is written in advance. The first two places are shared out according to placings in the Tour, the most popular riders in the race, and to the local champion, who's given the right to show himself off. Places three to five are sorted out during the race and an amateur is generally allowed to get in the next five to please the local supporters."

Of an event in 1995 he remembered: "Laurent Jalabert was making his show. He had just finished fourth in the Tour de France and he had the green jersey on his shoulders, with a win at Mende on July 14 [Bastille Day, the French holiday] as a bonus. Naturally the public wanted to see him in action.

"That day, though, nothing went the way it was planned. At the moment Jaja was supposed to drop back to us and the bunch was riding as a group to get up to him, his lead went up by a second a lap. Some riders started getting worried and complaints started flying. He wasn't respecting the rules. In the end a rider feigned a puncture and so he could wait for him and calm him down a bit. But when Jalabert got up alongside him, Jaja said to him: 'What are you talking about? I've been waiting for you for the last ten laps!'"

Another inside snippet from Menthéour: riders have been known to jump off and hide for a lap when the course goes into the countryside and there are no spectators to see them. Menthéour said: "In this job there are certain forbidden things that can be allowed under certain conditions. Crunching a lap [cycling slang for skipping one] is allowed. Provided you've just had a good Tour de France."

Menthéour, however, tried it going through a forest in the Bol d'Or des Monédières at Chaumeuil in France. He hadn't had a good Tour de France. He wasn't even that much of a rider, at least so far as his record went. That day, he says, he was having a hard time as the Swiss star, Tony Rominger, pushed up the pace. He stopped among the trees, took a flechette [shortened hypodermic] of amphetamine from his pocket and injected himself in the shoulder before jumping back in next lap. The riders weren't upset that he had drugged himself. That, says Menthéour, was permitted. What wasn't allowed was to take time off when your reputation didn't justify it.

"In this world of hypocrisy," he said, "there was hell to pay."

43

HOW TO BE JUST A LITTLE TOO GOOD (2)

Switzerland, a little country of mountains where you'd think people would steer clear of bikes, has a striking record in cycling. In the 1950s, for instance, it had the elegant Hugo Koblet, the epitome of sleekness, the dark ski goggles wound around one of his long arms, an image of playboy elegance. And it also had the heaving, sweating, foaming Ferdy Kübler, a man as wild and entertaining as Koblet was smooth.

Kübler, never a comfortable speaker of French, nevertheless used it to the point of being annoying. He would often drop back to the team cars and reporters following the Tour and perhaps slap his thighs and shout "Ferdy big horse today; Ferdy do big things" before riding back up to the group. Usually it just amused, all the more for being oddly phrased in elementary French. But sometimes it also annoyed. On one Tour he dropped back repeatedly to Raphaël Géminiani, the former rider who was managing a French team.

"Ferdy strong today. Ferdy attack soon. French boys ready?" he'd say. And then, a few minutes later: "France strong for Ferdy? Ferdy go soon. France strong enough?"

And so it would go on, the not always patient and undemonstrative Géminiani getting increasingly irritated in the heat of the team car and at yet another burst of bad French from the eccentric Swiss. Finally he let him boast once more of how he would soon ride away so strongly that the French couldn't follow before leaning out of the car and replying in deliberately equally bad French: "Ferdy shut up now or Ferdy get head knocked in."

By contrast, Koblet's trademarks were a comb, sponge and small bottle of cologne that he carried in a narrow extra pocket sewn into the back of his jersey. He would take his hands from the bars before the finish and run the comb through his thinning hair, then wipe his face with the cologne before crossing the line. He was then ready to meet his public. The showmanship brought him the nickname Pedaller of Charm from the French singer Jacques Grello, who saw him win alone at Agen in the 1951 Tour, going through his grooming routine as Fausto Coppi, Louison Bobet, Gino Bartali and others struggled to catch him. Koblet had the time to do it: he won by 2:25 after riding alone for 135 km.

The people who loved it most were his fans and the journalists. And, frankly, that was probably for whom he did it, to build his image. But it could sometimes have a devastating effect on his rivals. In the 1951 Tour of Switzerland, for instance, he was having a hard time in the mountains from the Frenchman François Mahé. Unable to stay alongside him, let alone attack him, he opted for psychological warfare instead. When Mahé was riding his hardest, Koblet took his hands off the bars and started combing his hair. Mahé was so dispirited that he gave up and dropped back.

Koblet stopped racing in 1958, sadly a shadow of the man he'd been. He spent his money on a convivial lifestyle, including a tour of the Americas in the hope of refinding his health. His debts grew, his wife left him. On November 2, 1964, his white Alfa-Romeo left a bend just outside Zürich and crashed into a pear tree. The speed—120 km/h—was shown by the jammed speedometer.

He died three nights later, aged 39.

44

HOW NOT TO CHAT UP A SUPER-STAR

The difference between being just an ordinary rider (nice guy, amateur sprinter, unknown) and Bernard Hinault (hard guy, professional roadman, internationally famous) is whether women come to you or you go to women. In Hinault's case, women came to him. Or one woman, anyway.

Bernard Hinault lives way out in the Brittany countryside but it's not hard to find his house because you have only to ask. That's the point about being well known. And ask is exactly what a girl did after Hinault retired from the Tour in 1980. He describes her as young, dirty and with long black hair, with an Indian look to her face. She spoke no French and Hinault speaks no other language so his wife, Martine, came down to try to decipher what she wanted.

At first the girl couldn't make herself understood and Martine despaired of her and went off to the garage to put dirty clothing into the washing machine. Hinault was left alone with his visitor. The girl then became more animated and, with sign language and a lot of physical actions, demanded he make love with her there and then.

"Just like that, completely matter of fact," was how he described it.

He turned her down and called his wife, which made the girl so angry that she began swearing angrily and hurling insults at him in Dutch. Hinault, as I said, speaks only French. He certainly doesn't speak Dutch. But he said afterwards that he recognised the language and that he knew she was swearing dreadfully … because he'd heard Dutch riders use the same words in races. "I'd spent enough time with Dutch riders in the peloton to get the general drift," he said. "I showed her the door without more ado. She departed on foot, carrying her luggage in a polyethylene carrier."

45

HOW TO STAY CLEAR OF THE LAW

If you started this book at the beginning and you've read it all the way through, you'll remember an old chap called Norbert Peugeot. If, on the other hand, you've been frivolously reading some chapters and skipping others, you may not know who he is. In which case, you have no option but to go back to the start and begin all over again; book editors pay by the word and they hate it when authors repeat themselves. When you've caught up with old Norbert, come back here and I'll pick up the story.

You've done that? Right ... here we go, then.

Norbert's tactic worked and the 1907 Paris–Roubaix was won by one of his riders, a man with a wide mouth and a stumpy chin, called Georges Passerieu. Peugeot had high hopes for him because he'd come second in the previous year's Tour de France even though he'd turned professional only a few months earlier. The trouble was that riding behind motorbikes in track races made him very fast but useless as a sprinter. The team therefore decided that he should wait until the race got close to Roubaix and then go for a solo bolt for the line.

Obediently, Passerieu got to Douai with a group of favourites and then left them, holding his lead to Roubaix. He was exhausted and filthy and looked in desperate happiness at the track gates ahead of him. He had only to ride through them, turn right, ride a lap ... and win the great new spring classic that had caught France's imagination.

And what happened? He was just meters from the gates when out into the road stepped a stern-looking policeman, his hand turned flat into Passerieu's face. Stop! But what terrible thing had he done? Or had there been a fire in the track, perhaps, or a riot, something that stopped his going in? Was there bad news from home that the policeman had to pass on immediately? All that was going through

Passerieu's exhausted mind as he pulled to a halt with his brakes rubbing on their grubby rims.

The policeman stood impassive until he'd stopped, then examined his bike with care. When he was satisfied, he waved the winner of Paris–Roubaix on his way. Passerieu swore, but not badly enough to be arrested all over again, and started his worn-out legs on to the last meters of his long journey.

And what had been so grave as to bring the great race to a stop, to put the winner's victory in peril? The licence plate. In those days Frenchmen had to spend a few sous each year on a licence for their bike and the policeman had waited for hours to check that Passerieu had one. The law was not to be mocked, even by the greatest riders in the world. Not in Roubaix, anyway.

Luckily, there's a happy ending. Passerieu won Paris–Roubaix, although he was only just crossing the line when the second man arrived.

Finish-line commotion like that is nothing new in Paris–Roubaix. In 1903 the wonderfully named Hippolyte Aucouturier was approaching the finish with two other riders, Claude Chapperon and Louis Trousselier (the soldier who gambled away all his prizes). They had been away for much of the race.

In those days the rule for races finishing on vélodromes was that riders would drop their road bikes at the entrance and jump on to fixed-gear and brakeless machines more usually used on a track. In Paris–Roubaix they would then ride three laps of the track and sprint for the line.

Helpers stood at the stadium entrance ready to hand over the new bikes but confusion broke out and Chapperon grabbed Trousselier's bike by mistake. Trousselier wasn't happy to ride Chapperon's machine instead and the two men began a tugging match. Aucouturier rode away from both of them in the confusion and won by 90 meters. The following year, to add to the catalogue of odd finishes, he won again—but at such high speed that only 20 spectators got to the track in time to see him.

46

HOW TO AVOID TROUBLING THE JUDGES

Some riders are successful, others are persistent. Just a few are persistently unsuccessful. Among them, with a record unlikely to be bettered, is the unfortunate Georges Goffin, from Liège in Belgium. Known also as Georges Nemo, he started the Tour in 1909, 1910 and 1911 and abandoned them all on the first day. If you wonder why you've never heard of him, well, that's the reason.

Close behind Goffin in the misfortune stakes comes Arne K. Jonsson, the pride of Denmark. He abandoned just two Tours—1959 and 1960—but with the distinction that in 1960 he didn't even get to the start line. Instead he stood sadly by the roadside and watched the Tour disappear into the distance, a race he would have ridden had he had some cycling shoes.

The Tour in Jonsson's days was for national teams, which allowed in a lot of riders who wouldn't have made it into conventional trade teams but which meant that many had to ride in hotchpotch groupings. Denmark, one of cycling's smaller nations, was one of those that couldn't raise a complete team by itself and so Jonsson and Bent Ole Retvig rode in 1959 in an international team.

Danish cycling was as short of money as the riders were and the pair joked that the free meals and hotels they got during the Tour made it cheaper than most of the other races they went to. Even so, Retvig lasted only until stage seven, Jonsson for two further days.

The international team was judged a success, though, and the two were picked again in 1960. Denmark's finest had no more money than they'd had the year before and so this time Jonsson, Retvig and another Dane, Leif Hammel, worked out a program of races which would each pay their expenses for the day and each get them one step nearer to the start of the Tour in Paris. The schedule worked so well that they arrived in Paris at midnight before the race, congratulating themselves on having got the whole way from Denmark without spending an unnecessary kroner and even making a slight profit. It was in that happy mood that they fell asleep in their hotel as one day passed into the next. Next morning, the first day of the Tour, they were less content: thieves had emptied their car.

The three borrowed all they needed, other teams and riders coming to their rescue, but Jonsson couldn't find any shoes that fitted. Inconsolable, he dropped out of the race without once turning a pedal. Of the others, Retvig got some shoes but not the right size and his feet began bleeding as they rubbed the sharp metal of his toe-clips. He pulled out, well behind the bunch, and forced his British team-mate Tony Hewson to pull out as well.

Hewson had ridden with Retvig the previous year and, feeling sorry for his Danish friend, had stopped to help him tend his bleeding feet. The rest of the race rode further and further ahead and by the time Retvig finally decided he wasn't going to continue, Hewson had no chance of getting back by himself and he was obliged to climb into the *voiture balai* in as depressed a mood as Retvig but feeling much more aggrieved. The remaining Dane, Hammel, lasted five days.

If, all these years later, you happen to spot the names Jonsson and Retvig on building complexes on the French Riviera, that's them. They went into business there when their careers were over. The last I heard, they were still there.

47

HOW TO PICK UP A SOUVENIR

Everyone likes a good day out, and a trip to the Tour de France is better than most. So many people stand by the roadside that they become not just a blur to the riders but their numbers are so great that they're supposed to cause a dip in the French economy for the three weeks they take off to see their heroes. It's a nice story but in fact most of the French nation goes on holiday in July or August so, even if they weren't standing beside the road or watching their televisions, many of them wouldn't have been at work regardless.

One 15-year-old had his special day on July 3, 1994. He was a member of the bike club at Roubaix, which was riding to three of the stage towns that the Tour would use that year in northern France. That took them to Armentières. What they saw was much more than the bunch sprint they expected. They were at first amused and then horrified to see one of the policemen guarding the spectators' barrier take out a small camera and step into the road for the perfect close-up snap. Both his view and his concentration distracted by the camera, he stepped into the path of the Belgian, Wilfried Nelissen, who had the Frenchman, Laurent Jalabert, right behind him.

Nelissen hit the policeman full on. His bike reared into the air and brought down Jalabert, who landed on his face and needed a hospital operation. Nelissen broke a collar bone. The young man from Roubaix was torn between shock and concern for Nelissen and Jalabert, who had become the darling of France and his personal hero, and the moment of opportunism that attracts any 15-year-old.

"I don't know what came over me," he recalled eight years later when he had himself become rather better known. "I've collected souvenirs all my life so when the policeman's camera fell to the ground and broke open, I saw the batteries rolling along the ground and picked them up." He took the batteries home, showed them to his friends and put them away somewhere safe. For all I know, he has them to this day.

Now, though, they have to compete with more important souvenirs and bigger memories. Because the fresh-faced boy who stretched out for the batteries as the ambulance men tended to Jalabert and Nelissen was called Arnaud Tournant. It was a name known then only to his friends and family. In 2001, though, he held three world championships and became the world's first man to ride a kilometer in less than a minute.

With a pleasing roundness to the tale, Tournant had just reached the peak of his career when Jalabert was ending his. In 2002 Jaja said farewell to the Tour de France while wearing the polkadot jersey of mountain king, having concentrated on climbing rather than sprinting ever since the disaster at Armentières. That autumn Jalabert left his home near Geneva for his last race, the world championship at Zolder in Belgium, and gave a farewell hug to his wife, Sylvie, who had presented him his bouquet when he won his first ever race.

"Hey," he said, "the next time I see you, I won't be a racing cyclist any more."

48

HOW TO WIN THE YELLOW JERSEY ... RELUCTANTLY

The yellow jersey is the greatest symbol that a cyclist can wear. It has never been copyrighted, its origins are far from clear, but such is its power that everyday cyclists in France are reluctant to wear too much yellow for fear that they commit sacrilege. That makes it all the odder that the two men with a claim to having worn the first one should have thought so badly of it.

The first yellow jersey was either Eugène Christophe on July 18, 1919, or Philippe Thys of Belgium six years earlier in 1913. Christophe's claim is undeniable because there are pictures of him wearing it, not least on the front cover of *La Vie au Grand Air*, the first time the *maillot jaune* had ever been pictured in colour. But he didn't like wearing it and spectators thought he looked as comical as he felt and they kept shouting "Canary!" as he passed.

Legend says the jersey was yellow to match the paper that *L'Auto*, the organising newspaper, used to distinguish it from the green of its rival, *Vélo*. Equally probable is that it was the only colour available in the shortages that followed the first world war, that the Tour had ordered jerseys from Paris and that the only colour the supplier had in large quantities at late notice was unpopular yellow.

Philippe Thys on the other hand said that he wore a yellow jersey in 1913, half a decade before Christophe.

Thys, from Anderlecht in Brussels, was the first man to win three Tours, in 1913, 1914 and 1920. When he was 67 he told the magazine *Champions et Vedettes* that Henri Desgrange had asked him to wear a distinctive colour as race leader but that he hadn't wanted to be more visible to rivals. Then his manager at Peugeot, Alphonse Baugé, had persuaded him that a yellow jersey would be a good advertisement for the company and he was obliged to concede.

Thys recalled: "A yellow jersey was bought in the first shop we came to. It was just the right size, although we had to cut a slightly larger hole for my head to go through."

The Tour's own historians take the claim seriously, saying Thys was "a valorous rider ... well known for his intelligence" and that his memories "seem free from all suspicion." But they can't find newspaper cuttings or records—most of the Tour's paperwork disappeared in the war—to prove his story. Nevertheless, Thys's claim becomes more convincing because of the detail that, the following year, "I won the first stage and was beaten by a tire by Bossus in the second. On the following day the *maillot jaune* passed to Émile Georget after a crash." So Christophe, far from being the first maillot jaune, may not even have been the second. The yellow jersey may have been a short-lived novelty that was temporarily forgotten until it was revived for Christophe half a decade later. Only then did it take on its modern significance.

However reluctant both the original claimants may have been, their unhappiness was nothing compared to the permanently morose Italian, Andrea Carrea, rider number 24 in 1952. Poor little Carrea, a man unblessed by the gods of good looks—he had a long thin face, a prominent chin, jug ears, thinning hair and a great rudder of a nose that pointed down at the end like a snout—was a domestique in the Italian national team. It was in that role that Fausto Coppi told him to join a break of three that went clear on the stage from Mulhouse to Lausanne, to keep an eye on it and above all to do nothing to make it go faster.

Obediently, Carrea joined in and did nothing to make it go faster. He didn't need to: it went so fast that it got to Lausanne five minutes ahead of the field even without his help. The little-known Walter Diggelmann won the stage after 239 km and almost seven and a half hours of racing—but Carrea got the yellow jersey. He was terrified. And, far from happy, he burst into sobs and refused to go to the podium. He got there only after officials pushed him there.

Carrea had never intended to lead the Tour de France. This was a man who cleaned and polished Fausto Coppi's shoes every morning, who not only sought no personal success but was scared of having it. And now he had not only beaten his leader but he was about to wear the yellow jersey … a jersey he had taken from another Italian, Fiorenzo Magni. He received his winner's bouquet with the same enthusiasm as men had once received the guillotine on the back of their neck.

The legendary French journalist Pierre Chany wrote: "At last the peloton put in an appearance, among the riders being Coppi and Magni. When the latter spotted Carrea decked in yellow he scowled, and the new leader's teeth began to chatter. Then Coppi slowly finished his ride. He pointed at Carrea and burst into deep laughter. Only then did the poor fellow start waving his bouquet and smiling at the photographers.

"Next morning Carrea was up early and began his day, as usual, by cleaning Coppi's shoes. Later the *campionissimo* overwhelmed the opposition on the Alpe d'Huez and put everything back into proper order."

Carrea never won a stage, never rode the Tour again, although he did finish ninth in the year he was the Tour's most unhappy *maillot jaune*. He looked as gloomy at the end as he had been throughout.

49

HOW TO WATCH A HORROR MOVIE

Leni Riefenstahl died in 2003, when she was 101. If the name sounds familiar, it's because she made a dramatic film of the 1936 Olympics, when they were held in Berlin. She didn't stint herself because she used 30 cameramen and 300,000 meters of film, three-quarters of which were unusable. The rest, though, she turned into *Olympische Spiele 1936,* one of the most striking sports films ever made.

Many people have criticised it, and her, for apparent lauding of Adolf Hitler and National Socialism. But Guy Lapébie was less interested in all that when he sat down to watch it than he was in seeing what Riefenstahl had got of him in the bike race.

Lapébie was the younger, weaker but much more pleasant of two French brothers who rode the Tour de France. Roger, a difficult, argumentative type, rode five times before the war and came third in 1934; Guy also came third, but after the war, in 1948. On the other hand Roger went better by actually winning in 1937.

Anyway, Guy had gone out for the night to watch Riefenstahl's film and after a lot of dramatic shots of divers and runners, there he was in the finish of the road race on the Avus car circuit on the capital's outskirts. The race was just 100 km and the circuit was easy, so the pace had been fast but there'd been little action. It was going to be a sprinters' finish.

Lapébie realised that and on the run to the line he'd got himself in front at exactly the right moment. And then, with 30 meters to go, he slowed down suddenly. Another Frenchman, Robert Charpentier, went by him and got the gold medal. Lapébie came second, timed in 0.2 seconds slower, his front tire just a little behind the back one of Charpentier.

Until the night he saw the film, Lapébie had never understood how it happened, how Charpentier had come past him. And then, suddenly, he knew. Because there on the screen he could see his teammate grabbing his shorts and giving him a good tug backwards. He felt, understandably, not only cheated but furious. He'd never liked Charpentier, a man often described as lighthearted, immensely self-confident and as strong as an ox.

The words "immensely self-confident" are usually taken to mean arrogant and boasting. And Charpentier was arrogant and he boasted. Even when he went out training with the boys on Sundays, he would brag: "I am going to break away at kilometer 85; follow me if you can."

Clearly, to Lapébie's mind, this Charpentier just couldn't stand being beaten, not by a fellow Frenchman and least of all in the Olympic road race. Journalists watching the race had already had their doubts and now Lapébie could point to what he saw as the evidence. "I was tugged backwards at the last moment," he said. "From the day I saw that film, I considered myself the moral victor of the Olympic Games."

Well, Charpentier wasn't going to take that lying down. He was furious. "That is the biggest lie I have ever heard," he stormed. "I'll sue Lapébie for defamation even if it costs me a month's wages!" Well, the row entertained French cycling for ages, both riders and their supporters and even some who hadn't previously been interested starting to salivate at this battle of the bitching stars, with each side getting ever angrier. Finally both sides realised there was going to be a lot more snorting than actual action and that they would have to race together in the future. Best that they called a truce. Lapébie told the magazine *Miroir des Sports* that he had been misquoted, it always being easy to blame the journalist, and that what he'd actually said was that he had been tugged. He hadn't, he said, claimed specifically that it was Charpentier who did it.

That ended the matter, at least so far as the claims and counter-claims were concerned, but it's doubtful the pair ever got on well again. The French journalist René de Latour said of the incident: "What I saw of the finish was Charpentier jerking out of the blue, with Lapébie trying to match him. To me, it seemed the neatest sprint in the world."

But then again, de Latour wasn't as close to the action as Lapébie had been. Nor as Charpentier had been. Nor did he have the advantage that you have now, that you can watch the film on video and run it backwards and forwards and at full speed and very slowly. You should try that one day. Maybe it will tell you whether Guy Lapébie really did see what he claimed he saw in the darkness of the cinema that day, whether he was cheated or not from his medal. And since Lapébie is often to be seen by the roadside when the Tour finishes at Bordeaux, near his home, you could perhaps ask a little moment of his time and tell him what you've seen. Provided you agree that he was cheated, of course. He may not want to know otherwise.

50

HOW TO STRUGGLE ON BRAVELY

It is the most open Tour de France for years. The favorite has weakened. A promising outsider of the same nationality sees his chance. Then he falls. He breaks his collar bone but doctors strap him up so that he can barely move but he can carry on riding. He is in terrible pain, but this is the Tour de France and he struggles on regardless. Not only does he carry on riding, but he wins the admiration and sympathy of the watching world for his courage and his terrible suffering.

Sound familiar? Of course, it does. But you think this is about Tyler Hamilton in 2003, don't you? It's not. It's about Pascal Simon, exactly 20 years earlier. But you can be sure that nobody showed a greater personal interest in the American's own bravery.

Our story starts not in France but Spain. Miguel Indurain is about to win the amateur championship. And it is the first year of Felipe Gonzaléz's socialist government, which may seem dull to you but was anything but to the Spanish after so many decades of fascist dictatorship.

May 8 was a busy day in 1983. There was mass in the morning, then another election and then an afternoon of fun. For the people of Madrid that meant the finish of the Vuelta downtown. They'd have liked a Spanish winner but they seemed happy to have Bernard Hinault. After Spain, many expected him to win a fifth Tour de France that summer, because in those days the Vuelta was always before the Tour and not, as now, at the end of the season.

It wasn't to be. Hinault suffered in Spain, in pain from his right knee. It was a return of the misery that had forced him to vanish from the Tour late one night in 1980. On the days that Hinault struggled, he was helped by a serious, bespectacled team-mate from the edge of

Paris, a man called Laurent Fignon. He had just turned 23 and he'd been racing for just seven years, having until then played soccer. He won his first race as an amateur and in 1982, a year before the Vuelta, he turned professional for Renault. Quite a talent, therefore, but as yet untested in the Tour.

Before the Vuelta, nobody doubted who would lead the yellow and black troops of Renault and their Gitane bikes in the world's biggest race. That would be Hinault. (As an aside, since Renault and Gitane were owned by the French state, Hinault and Fignon weren't simply professional cyclists but civil servants.) But Hinault couldn't start and so Fignon the super-domestique and second-year pro found himself heading the team that France counted on to win.

It wasn't going to be easy. A lot of riders saw Hinault's absence as their own chance. Whole teams saw their opportunity. Among them, Peugeot in their white and checkered jerseys. Their best rider turned out to be Pascal Simon, a man with a long bony face. From third place on the 10th stage, he got into a group on the stage that went over the Tourmalet, Aspin and Peyresourde. The winner was Robert Millar, who broke away on the Peyresourde in his first Tour and won by six seconds.

But he wasn't the only Peugeot rider on the rostrum. Because after him, up stepped Simon to accept the yellow jersey. You can imagine the joy in the Peugeot hotel that night. Stage winner, race leader … and Laurent Fignon, the great hope of the Renault team, four and a half minutes down.

Oh, they were happy. And then the party went cold. Next day, Simon touched wheels and fell on to rock. The medical team, led by Gérard Porte, was with him quickly. Simon thought it was his collar bone and he insisted on carrying on. Struggling on, in fact, constantly in pain, his eyes ringed with tears, not just for a day but almost a week.

"You don't abandon the Tour de France," he said. "It's so hard to come back if you do. You drop out only if you're really forced to … or if your name is Petacchi" (the Italian sprinter who gave up in 2003 after dominating the start of the Tour à la Cipollini). "If you're French, it means so much to get to the Champs Elysées."

Simon didn't get there. After keeping his yellow jersey for six days, an enormous bandage round his shoulder and with only one arm he could use, he came to the côte de la Chapelle after 99 km. It was nothing like the Alpe d'Huez which finished the stage. But it was too much. He pulled one foot off its pedal and put it to the ground, his body to the handlebars, his eyes weeping.

"I was five minutes behind the peloton," he says. "There was no point in carrying on suffering. But somehow, when you stop, the pain gets worse. It's bad when you finish a race, but it's worse when you give up before the end. And physically, people tell you it'll get better with time, day by day. But it never stops. You can never forget it. Every time you brake hard, it throws you forward on to the bars. Every bend, every bump in the road, it's the same. You don't know your limits until you're sick."

He became one of a surprisingly long list of riders to abandon while leading. The first was Francis Pélissier, who fell ill in 1927, followed by Victor Fontan who in 1929 had to hunt from door to door for a spare bike (his broadcast sobbing changed the rules denying riders the help of mechanics). Belgium's Sylvère Maes went home in 1937, angry with French spectators, and Fiorenzo Magni packed his bags in 1950 in sympathy with Gino Bartali, who insisted—wrongly—that a spectator had threatened him with a knife.

Wim van Est went home in 1951 after falling over the edge of the col d'Aubisque, Bernard van de Kerckhove fell sick in 1971, Luis Ocaña crashed on the col de Mente in 1971. Then Michel Pollentier was caught defrauding the dope check after winning the yellow jersey on Alpe d'Huez in 1978. Knee troubles forced out Bernard Hinault in 1980, Rolf Sorensen broke his collar bone in 1991, Stéphane Heulot pulled out with tendinitis of a knee in 1996, and Chris Boardman hit an Irish wall in 1998.

Simon's retirement meant Fignon won the Tour at his first attempt. It made him the arithmetical equal of Jean Robic in 1947, Fausto Coppi in 1949, Hugo Koblet in 1951, Jacques Anquetil in 1957, Felice Gimondi in 1965, Eddy Merckx in 1969, and Bernard Hinault in 1979.

But he had profited from the misfortune not simply of a rival but of a superior. Would he have won had Simon not crashed? There's no point in guessing, is there?

As for Simon, he rode the Tour every year until 1991. Then he called his career to an end the day after Paris–Tours, which he finished an unnoticed 147th. But there was a final smile. In 2001, a decade after Pascal stopped racing, his brother François also became *maillot jaune*. And not just that but right there on Alpe d'Huez, the mountain his brother never reached. That day Pascal drove through the night to join him there. And there they celebrated just as Peugeot had celebrated that yellow jersey 20 years earlier.

It exorcised a lot of devils in Pascal's mind.

LaVergne, TN USA
26 August 2010
194758LV00006B/2/P

9 780984 311712